Janet g

FROM: Scotbec

December 1978

Crafts of the
Highlands and Islands

Crafts of the Highlands and Islands

John Manners

David & Charles

Newton Abbot · London
North Pomfret (Vt) · Vancouver

*All photographs are by the
author*

British Library Cataloguing in Publication Data
Manners, John Errol
   Crafts of the Highlands and Islands.
   1. Handicraft - Scotland - Highlands
   I. Title
   680   TT61

ISBN 0-7153-7485-0

Library of Congress Catalog Card Number 77-91719

Typeset by HBM Typesetting Limited Chorley Lancashire
and printed in Great Britain
by Biddles Limited Guildford Surrey
for David & Charles (Publishers) Limited
Brunel House Newton Abbot Devon

Published in the United States of America
by David & Charles Inc
North Pomfret Vermont 05053 USA

Published in Canada
by Douglas David & Charles Limited
1875 Welch Street North Vancouver BC

Contents

Introduction 7

1 **Crofters** 11

2 **Boatbuilders** 14

3 **Woodworkers** 18
Orkney Chairs

4 **Metalwork** 23
The Blacksmith · The Farrier · The Coppersmith

5 **Working with Stone** 27
Ballachulish Slates · Caithness Slabs · Portsoy Marble ·
Stone Walls

6 **Straw and Heather** 33
Basket Making · Rope Making · Thatching

7 **Hide and Horn** 39
Saddlery · Sheepskins · Deerskins · Hornwork ·
Shepherd's Crooks

8 **Wool** 46
Milling · Weaving · Harris Tweed · Knitting ·
Shetland Shawls · Kilt Making

9 **Coopering** 65
Whisky Barrels · Fish Barrels

10 **Proceeds from the Sea** 71
Drying Fish · Salted Herrings · Kippers · Smokies ·
Finnan Haddock · Other Smoked Fish · Lobsters ·
Seaweed

11 **Proceeds from the Land** 80
Peat Digging · Corn Milling · Malting Barley ·
Whisky Distilling · Cheese Making

12 **Sporting Equipment**   90
   Fishing Rods · Fishing Flies · The Gunsmith
13 **Weapons and Instruments**   95
   Highland Fighting Equipment · Bagpipes · Fiddles
14 **Artist Crafts**   101
   Glassblowing · Glass Engraving · Pottery · Silverwork ·
   Pewterware · Bookbinding · Enamelling · Model Making ·
   Ships in Bottles
   Appendices   1 Craftsmen at Work   119
                    2 Crafts on Display   121
                    3 Addresses of Organisations   124
   Bibliography   125
   Index   127

Introduction

The primary object of this book has been to record in words and photographs the traditional crafts of the Scottish Highlands and Islands, many of which are disappearing or have already done so. In recent years, however, there has been an influx of artist trained craftsmen who have set up their workshops in the region, and some of these are also included.

I have taken 'the Highlands' to be the area north of the geological fault that runs from Dumbarton diagonally across Scotland to Stonehaven, just south of Aberdeen. This was the Highland line laid down by decree at the end of the eighteenth century, and covers a more extensive area than that which comes under the jurisdiction of the present-day Highlands and Islands Development Board.

The clearances of the eighteenth century had a very great effect on the people of the Highlands. To enable the landowners to keep vast flocks of sheep, the crofters were dispossessed of their homes and had no option but to move to the coastal areas or to emigrate.

The central Highlands, although they look attractive enough to the holiday visitor, are for the most part inhospitable to the farmer. Apart from their use for sheep rearing, the once bare hills are being planted with trees — mostly introductions from abroad and nearly all conifers, with sitka spruce predominating. Forestry is a very big industry, growing in importance.

In an effort to stem the continuing slow drift away from the Highlands and Islands, communications have been improved by the building of new roads or expansion of existing ones, and electricity has been brought to all crofts, however remote. Grants and loans are available for people to establish or develop business concerns — an attractive proposition for the dedicated craftsman, whether artist or traditional, to 'get away from it all' and set up a workshop in peaceful surroundings.

The development of the oil industry has had its effect on crafts in the Highlands. Young men can earn large sums of money for any work connected with oil, such as shipping, construction and all the ancillary businesses. This makes it more difficult for the old master craftsmen to obtain and keep apprentices.

Fortunately, in the Shetlands, the Sollum Voe oil complex is a fair way from any town, and in the Orkneys oil activities are confined to the island of Flotta. Consequently, in the Islands, there is not much disruption in the local economy, while the benefits are being used to improve community facilities.

Here, crofters were at one time almost self-sufficient and the few things they wanted were normally obtained by trucking or bartering. They were jacks-of-all-trades, capable of thatching, building stone walls, spinning and weaving.

A significant feature of the whole area is the scarcity of wood. Hardly a tree is to be seen in the Shetlands and Outer Hebrides, and very few in the Orkneys. Trees cannot stand the high winds of these exposed islands. Wood was therefore very valuable; it had to be imported by the fishing boats or collected from the shore by beachcombing. Peat was used as fuel.

Today oil presents the most likely key to the region's prosperity and, with better communications, there has been a huge increase in the number of tourists during the comparatively short summer season.

The crafts that are just surviving are basket making with straw; thatching, hand spinning and weaving, and coopering for herring barrels.

Boatbuilding is having a slump in the Islands, but along the north-east coast of the mainland all the yards seem to be constructing new boats.

8

Saddlery is carried on, but with so few saddlers it is difficult to meet the increasing demand for this work.

Whisky distilling, barley malting, and coopering for whisky barrels are now thriving, after a rather sticky period.

Of the many artist craftsmen who have started up in business, a number are doing extremely well, though there seems to be a fairly high wastage rate. It takes time, hard work, skill and a certain flair for a business to prosper, and building up a reputation can be a slow process.

This type of craftsman seems able to survive in some very out of the way places, such as the colony at Balnakiel, in an old wartime camp; others are in even more remote localities. Disused railway stations are favoured by some, notably at Dess, Crathes, and Dornoch, where they thrive, though this is largely due to the skill and originality of the particular craftsmen.

There is a special Highland Trade Fair at Aviemore where craftsmen can show their wares. Their main outlet, however, is in the numerous craft shops. A great many of these display work of a very high standard, although poor quality and trivial items do creep in sometimes; and some shops sell a lot of foreign imports as well.

These shops offer a wide range of fine tweeds and tartans; knitted garments, mostly in the Fair Isle style; Caithness glass, in particular paper weights of really exceptional quality; cast silver work; pottery, antler work, woodwork and lapidary, as well as a variety of trinkets.

The craft scene is thus a very varied one; artist craftsmen have to be businessmen to survive, while the crofter is often confused by inflation and does not know what price to ask for his crafts. He usually tends to undercharge and many of his products that reach the market make a profit for others while he remains comparatively poor. For these traditional craftsmen, however, it is the skills that are important — perhaps the sense of achievement is even more satisfying than the financial reward.

1 Crofters

A crofter is someone who occupies a croft — a holding of farm-land varying from just a few acres to around forty or more. There are 19,000 crofts in the Highlands but only 16,000 crofters, as some of the old farmsteads are derelict and land is more in demand than housing. Crofters tend to be very versatile, as it is rarely possible to make a living from the croft alone. Thus some are labourers; in the outer Hebrides many are weavers; in the Shetlands they are fishermen with a croft, and in the more fertile Orkneys they are crofters with a fishing boat. In the past a crofter built his own house, thatched the roof, mended the dry stone walls, tanned skins and dug peat; occasionally he had the skill to build a boat, but would turn his hand to any job available. His wife looked after the animals and croft when he was away fishing; she also dried fish and sheep meat for winter use, spun the wool and made the yarn for weaving or knitting. In addition to the land of the croft, the crofters frequently had grazing rights on the scattalds, or common lands, which are a feature of the Shetlands and Fair Isle.

A curious fact is that while the crofter is usually only a tenant the house always belongs to him. In earlier times he could be evicted without compensation, but under the Crofters Act of 1886 he was given security; today, if he moves, he is recompensed for the value of his house. There are subsidies for land improvement, such as turning heather land into good pasture — as is being done on a sizeable scale in Lewis and the Shetlands. In Lewis, the crofters still retain the sheiling huts where they live in the summer months with their sheep.

The number of derelict crofts is particularly noticeable in the outlying islands. When left unoccupied, their thatched roofs soon disintegrate, leaving only the walls and chimneys standing. As they are almost impossible to modernise, more and more of these dwellings are falling into ruins.

The houses are mostly constructed like fortresses, especially in the islands where the winds are so fierce. Everything is built of stone, except for new buildings made of breeze block with cavity walls, rendered on the outside, and an imitation 'slate' roof of asbestos. The houses are frequently built by the dry stone wall method — without using mortar — but are normally plastered inside. The windows are very small or possibly non-existent, as in the black houses of Lewis. These are constructed with walls 3ft thick, of large stones outside and inside making a sandwich of the sand in the middle. The roof thatch only overlaps the inner wall and the rain-water seeps down through the filling of sand. This type of house is probably still lived in today and is certainly in use as a cow byre. Originally this dwelling had an outlet in the form of a louvre, or chimney, in the middle of the roof over a peat fire, and the smoke eventually found its way up and out.

A number of croft dwellings have been preserved as museums and these show the traditional features very well. The furnishings and fittings are much the same throughout: cooking utensils and pots, usually a display of farm implements, a spinning wheel, a fiddle and sometimes a set of bagpipes, a family Bible, some roughly made furniture, possibly constructed from driftwood, an oil light and sometimes a built-in bed with curtains all round. The houses are usually of the 'but and ben' type, consisting of a living room and a sleeping compartment with an earth floor.

The dwellings always have a cow byre, either as part of the house or erected nearby. Many also had a grain dryer in a small circular building and rotary hand querns to grind the corn. Close to the homestead, there was always a kale or potato patch

A croft with everything — electricity, television and a car.

heavily walled to keep out the agile sheep. Now that electricity has been connected to all the crofts, there is often the incongruous sight of a television aerial protruding above the thatched roof.

2 Boatbuilders

The building of wooden fishing boats has long been an important craft industry in the Islands and on the north-east coast of
Scotland, but at the present time, while the small yards on the
mainland are mostly doing reasonably well, there is little work
for boatbuilders on the Islands.

There has been a steady falling off in the number of smaller
inshore fishing boats over the years, as the waters have become
overfished and the herring catch has declined so disastrously.
A few boats are used for lobsters and crabs, which are caught in
creels and then flown to the Continent. These too are becoming
scarcer, though the smaller catches have been cushioned by
higher prices.

The normal boat of around 85ft with 100 tons displacement
costs between £300,000 and £400,000. Most of these are
privately owned, bought with the help of a loan and subsidy
from the White Fish Authority. It seems a lot of money, but
between £3,000 and £4,000 worth of fish a week can be landed,
occasionally over £20,000. Given reasonable luck, very much
depends on the ability of the skipper and how hard he is
prepared to work.

This type of boat takes about a year to build. It has massive
frames and a keel of oak with larch planking; the wood is used
green and unseasoned. The decks are usually of iroko, an
imported wood rather similar to teak. The curvature of the side
planking is achieved by steaming the wood, which becomes
quite pliable and easy to work. These planks are about $2\frac{1}{2}$in

thick and are fixed on by 6in galvanised nails. The completed boat is fitted with a powerful diesel engine, radar, wireless, an echo-sounding machine and a Decca navigator. These are sophisticated instruments and the successful skipper must be a man of considerable intelligence. The boat should have a working life of about twenty-five years, covering fifty weeks of the year, and undergoes a short annual refit. Normally this type of boat leaves port in the evening and stays out fishing overnight.

In the Islands subsidies and loans are harder to get. Very few new boats are being built in the Shetlands, but there are some in the Orkneys at Stromness, and one or two in the Outer Hebrides.

The fortunate few yards which have orders are building small, general purpose boats, with a large area around the stern to take the creels, when used for lobster fishing. These boats are generally built in the clinker style, with overlapping planks; some of them have a very long life and seldom need to be replaced. Fortunately there is always a certain amount of repair work to keep the yards going.

Cross-section of a wooden fishing boat under construction at Peterhead

The older men who build these boats do so with a remarkable degree of skill and work almost entirely by eye. Sometimes they have a jig to help them, but with years of practice they have acquired a degree of expertise that is extraordinary.

Wood is very expensive and variable in quality, and the boatbuilder cannot afford the luxury of having a big stock on hand. A typical yard to suffer from rising costs is James Duncan, of Burray Island in the Orkneys, who is the fifth generation of boatbuilders, with a large building shed and a good slipway. Shortage of orders has forced him to take on woodwork for buildings. He has the skill and versatility to carry out such jobs, but it is a poor substitute for boatbuilding.

An interesting newcomer to the industry is Halmatic Ltd, of Hatston just outside Kirkwall, which started business in its present factory in 1970, making commercial boats from fibreglass. This type of hull, commonly used for yachts, has the great advantage of cutting down the amount of maintenance needed; no repainting is necessary as the whole hull is impregnated with the chosen colour.

The boats are 24ft, 36ft or 56ft — the lengths can be varied slightly — and made in large moulds, which are kept ready and can be used repeatedly. The hulls are built up in skins or layers glued together until there are between six and twenty skins which can give a finished thickness of 1in. The decks are also of fibreglass, though marine plywood is normally used for the bulkhead partitions. The firm employs around twenty men and thus makes an important contribution to the economy of the Orkneys. The boats are fitted out at private yards — another benefit to the local industry.

Glassfibre boats used to be cheaper and easier to build than conventional wooden craft, but the dramatic increase in the cost of oil, from which the materials are derived, means that the price advantage has been lost. However, this type of boat has proved itself in service and some are being exported.

Another interesting concern is Ferro Cement Boats, of Scrabster near Thurso. It is surprising to learn that the building of cement boats has been going on for over a hundred years and is on the increase.

Boats of up to 40ft can be made in the yard. They are built on a mould over which two layers of meshed metal are laid. Along this length, high tensile steel bars are fixed, and finally a 1in-thick layer of concrete is added. The boat is fitted with watertight compartments. Though a little heavier than fibreglass, in the larger concrete boats weight is saved as there are no ribs. If damaged, the skin may be pushed in slightly and crack like an egg, but it can be very easily repaired. When finished, the concrete boat looks no different from one built of wood. The initial cost is slightly cheaper and there is also a saving on maintenance.

3 Woodworkers

The wood turners, carvers and furniture makers are not very numerous and are spread over a wide area. Their products are much sought after, however, and they are doing good business.

Arthur Sutherland, of Haster in Caithness, has been making furniture for about seventy years, turning out spinning stools with their carved and tapering backs, refectory tables and dram stools — in oak that is fumed in ammonia to give it a mature look.

Wood turners make such articles as fruit bowls, using elm, walnut and some imported woods; these are hard and have close grain that responds well to polish, giving a fine finish. A very popular combination of turning and carving goes into the making of moulds for butter or shortbread, usually with a carved thistle in the middle and a decorated carved edging. Beech and sycamore are the woods most favoured for this work having an attractive light colour that looks well in a kitchen.

All the good woodworkers are particular about the fine finish of their products, which are very smooth and polished with linseed oil or beeswax.

There are one or two carvers, such as the artist Derek Riley, of Cullen, whose versatility ranges from ornamental wood carving to woodcuts and printing. Reynold Eunson, who makes

Arthur Sutherland, furniture maker of Haster in Caithness, with samples of his work — a carved-back spinning stool and a dram stool

the framework for Orkney chairs, is likewise a high-class carver and does work for St Magnus Cathedral in Kirkwall.

Orkney Chairs

The Orkney chair is a unique piece of furniture made out of a combination of wood and straw. As there was virtually no local timber available, driftwood was frequently used. The older furniture was very rudely constructed, often by the crofter himself for his personal needs. Usually the chair legs were very short so that a seated person would be at a level below the smoke

An Orkney chair, with basket-work hood; Reynold Eunson is making the frame

Woodworker John Crichton, of Braemar, making shortcake moulds

which swirled around the upper part of the interior from the central open fire. To save the precious wood and add a modicum of comfort, straw was introduced as a back-rest; an elaboration of this was to extend it to form a hood.

The chairs are made in small numbers on the island of Westray, and by Reynold Eunson in Kirkwall. There is a steady demand for them at around £80, a price that constantly edges upwards, and a waiting time of two or three years.

The wooden framework, make by Reynold Eunson, is of Japanese oak with morticed and tenoned joints, the arms and back supports being screwed to the main frame. The oak is fumed in a chamber, using ammonia which gives it a mature look and deters woodworm. The curved back — in some models fitted with a hood — is made of straw (see page 21); this work is done on a part-time basis by a crofter.

Eunson employs a pensioner to help him but, in common with many other craftsmen, has no apprentice. In any trade, apprentices expect a high rate of pay and in many crafts do not earn their keep for some time. They need supervising and, for someone like Reynold Eunson, this cramps his freedom of action, particularly as he is also a very skilled sculptor and carver in wood — work that requires concentration with no interruptions.

4 Metalwork

The Blacksmith

At one time every rural community had its blacksmith, who was busy making and repairing farm equipment, fitting wheel bonds to carts and wagons, and perhaps doing wrought iron work as well. His smithy was a well-situated and relatively valuable property, housing his forge, a sizeable workshop and a wide selection of tools. It was often a father-to-son business and may have been in the family for a hundred years or more. The blacksmith was a vital member of the country scene and remains so today, though there are few enough still at work.

Those who survive are versatile in every kind of metalwork and their order books are full for months ahead. Many of them carry out their work in what is virtually a museum of bygones, the accumulation of implements and spare parts is often a revelation of the past. The anvil is generally antique and the leather bellows are operated by hand.

Some blacksmiths are so situated that they can undertake first-aid repair jobs to oil company equipment or, more generally, to road-construction machinery too costly to be allowed to stand idle for want of a speedy adjustment. Such assignments are better and more quickly paid than any carried out for local farmers and so tend to be given priority. Near the coast, the blacksmith may make creels for lobster catching. His metal frames are strong and longer lasting than the traditional creel fashioned from bent cane.

Though many blacksmiths are creative and inventive, they

have little time available for wrought iron work, so that there is not much in the way of decorative gates or screens in the Highlands. Some small items, like door knockers and ram's horn paper knives, are made. Demand for this kind of work is so great that one blacksmith in the Shetlands had to put a notice in the paper saying he could not take on any more orders until further notice.

In earlier years horses were brought to the smithy to be shod and some blacksmiths still do shoeing as a sideline, but now that the horse population is much depleted and spread thinly over a wide area the farrier must go to them, and this has largely become a separate occupation.

The Farrier

Wherever there are horses and ponies a farrier must be available. Horses need shoeing every four to six weeks, so he provides an essential service. But, working full time, he needs a horse population of about 150 to provide him with a living. His work entails a great deal of travelling which takes up much of his time. One farrier travels 1,000 miles a month, covering distances up to 90 miles from his home for the purpose of shoeing horses; another had to make a trip by plane to carry out a job.

There are still some horses at work on the land, and plenty are used for transporting deer during the stalking season. Pony trekking is increasingly popular, particularly during the summer months. Gymkhanas too are part of the country calendar of events. All these require the services of a farrier. Stalking ponies are usually fitted with a shoe that has a toe bar; this short piece of metal across the front doubles the life of the shoe as well as helping the pony keep its footing over scree and stony ground. Calkins, which protrude downwards from the back of the shoe, are also used.

Some farriers fit the shoes 'cold'; others have a portable forge in their car and heat the shoes in a propane gas oven. Ready-made shoes are more commonly in use today; these are adapted to fit individual horses.

The majority of the farriers at work are older men. New entrants will be needed to carry on the service but before they can practise they will have to pass a trade test to comply with recent government legislation.

In the Islands, the picture is rather different. The Shetlands have the densest pony population — about a thousand are carefully bred there for export and some are used in the bulb fields of Holland — but paradoxically no farrier is needed. The ponies remain unshod and their hooves require only an occasional trim. In the Orkneys and Hebrides a pony is hardly ever seen; if there is any shoeing to be done, one of the few black-smiths will oblige.

The blacksmith's anvil and tools have been handed down through several generations. Here, a farrier makes a 'hot' shoe

The Coppersmith

Coppersmithing is a skilled craft particularly important in the making of stills for distilling malt whisky. These are made of sheet copper to a design that has remained unchanged for a hundred years. Bulbous at the base, the still narrows towards the funnel which extends upwards, becoming narrower at the top before turning down to the cooling cylinder. Each is made individually to the specification of the distiller, and the shaping is done by hand.

The copper sheets are first annealed to soften them and some are put through a rolling machine to curve them. The remainder of the operation consists of heating the copper with a blow-lamp and beating it into shape with a wooden mallet until the curving is correct and all dents are smoothed out.

Stills used to be riveted together but are now electric welded. The still is pickled in acid to remove any scale, and hammer finished to give a shiny surface.

The firms that make them are at Rothes and Dufftown. Each still takes six skilled coppersmiths about six weeks to complete and will last around fifteen years. There is a steady demand which keeps these craftsmen busy.

5 Working With Stone

Ballachulish Slates

The making of Ballachulish slates is the only defunct craft to appear in this book. The quarry closed in 1955 after nearly 300 years, during which time a very large percentage of Scottish houses had roof coverings of these slates. They were also used extensively for paving and as headstones for graves. Dark grey blue in colour, the slates had a slight sparkle from the pyrites contained in them.

When the quarry was working at its peak about a hundred years ago, nearly 600 men were producing six million slates a year. The slate was obtained by blasting, then split with chisels and mallets, and finally trimmed square with a slater's knife. The finished slates were sorted into their various sizes, which were given such names as 'duchesses' and 'countesses' — the same nomenclature used for Cotswold stone roofing slates in England. Something like seven-eighths of the material was wastage and great piles of it are to be seen by the roadside and forming the breakwater by the village of Ballachulish.

The industry declined in the same way as it did in Wales. Every slate required individual attention and the rising cost of labour priced them out of the market. Substitute materials, serviceable but less pleasing, have taken their place, such as slate-coloured asbestos or concrete tiles of varying subdued shades.

The quarry — a large grey gash in the hillside above Balla-chulish — serves as a memorial to one of the greatest sources of fine slates in Britain.

Caithness Slabs

In the Caithness quarries the stone lies in horizontal strata and splits naturally and easily into large sheets between 1in and 4in thick. Every so often there are vertical cracks at distances varying from 2ft to several yards. The stone is split by inserting a wedge and hammering it until there is a crack wide enough

Caithness slabs being quarried for use as paving stones

to take a crowbar. By levering the bar a sizeable slab can be dislodged. The slabs are stacked according to thickness, ready for cutting.

Originally a power-driven saw was used, but this has been replaced by a circular saw with a diamond cutting edge that slices easily through the stone. The slabs can be polished if required.

There used to be a number of separate operations carried out by quarrymen at the stone face: cutters to cut the stone; dressers to split it with hammers and double-sided axes; classers to sort the slabs by thickness, and scuffers to flake off pieces and make the sides parallel.

From 1890 to 1905 the annual output of the quarries around Spital, ten miles south of Thurso, averaged 16,000 tons and gave employment to 500 men. At that time Thurso was a thriving port for the shipment of grain as well as exporting the slabs. Paving stones from the Caithness quarries were supplied in quantity to London and sent all over the world, to America, Australia and South Africa.

The stone could also be split into layers only $\frac{7}{8}$in thick and trimmed for use as roofing tiles, or as shed slabs $2\frac{1}{2}$ft square on cow byres. Many roofs in the area are tiled with these stones which are very durable; they are also heavy and need strong roof trusses. Numerous fields around the quarries are enclosed by stone slabs standing on end, with the bottom edge set in the ground, to form a wall.

With the advent of concrete paving, and the problems and costs of transport, the quarries gradually closed down — the last of them in 1935. One quarry opened up again in 1945 and has continued production in a small way ever since. The present-day requirement is for paving and floor stones to replace worn ones — as have recently been supplied to the Scottish National Gallery in Edinburgh; for roof tiles, and also polished stone to be made into fireplaces. There is enough business to keep the quarry ticking over, but transport charges are likely to prevent a revival on any large scale.

Portsoy Marble

This is a serpentine type of rock that appears as a small outcrop near the little fishing port of Portsoy in Banffshire. The material is attractively coloured in variations of grey and can be polished quite easily to a high degree that enhances its natural grain and general appearance. As it is comparatively soft, it can be drilled, cut to shape and made into attractive ornaments, or can be worked as a base for items of desk furniture, ash trays, cigarette lighters and all manner of ornamental objects which can be found in craft shops over a wide area.

Stone Walls

Stone walls or dry stone dykes are a common sight throughout the Highlands and Islands. They vary with the geology of the district and the sort of stone locally available. Traditionally the walls are built 'dry' — that is, without mortar — but nowadays, with road improvements and the need for new walling, the stones are often cemented together.

Dykeing was a profession and most of the large estates employed men to maintain the walls. Today they are kept in shape by farm workers. A certain amount of new walling is made necessary when a road is widened or a field entrance enlarged to admit a combine harvester. All crofters can build and repair stone walls and have been doing so for centuries. When looked after, they last for ever and many are of a very great age.

The best method is for two men to work together, one at each side of the wall. The skill is to pick a stone of the exact size and shape required as the wall is built up. In Caithness, where the stone splits in layers, very neat walls can be achieved; in other areas the stones are rounded and this makes the task far more difficult. Frequently a mallet or slater's axe will be used to trim stones into shape.

To build evenly, a template is needed; this is a wooden frame of the same dimensions as a cross section of the wall. Strings are

Dry stone walling in Caithness; the flat stones of this region, stacked without mortar, make a neat wall

run from the top and bottom of the frame to another several yards away, and the wall is built out to these measurements. Normally there is a foundation of about 1ft below the surface. The wall is broader at the bottom and slopes in towards the top. The outer sides are made as flush as possible and the middle section filled with rubble and smaller stones.

A line of coping stones may be placed vertically along the top to give a finish. In Argyll the walls are often capped with turves — one layer turf-side down, the top layer turf-side up. Extra heavy stones are used in Fair Isle for the construction of walls, to withstand the severity of the weather; lighter ones are blown down in the gales. In some areas, particularly the Outer Hebrides, one thickness of stones with gaps showing between them is a common feature; the reason for this, according to one theory, is that sheep will not risk surmounting such apparently frail structures.

Apart from marking boundaries, one of the main purposes of the walls is to enclose livestock. Sheep and rams in particular are extremely agile and a high wall, frequently topped with a row of barbed wire, is necessary to keep them in. In the Shetlands, sheep can be seen wearing a wooden triangle around their necks to stop them penetrating barbed-wire fences.

In the north of Caithness, a different kind of stone wall is a common sight around fields. The local slab stones are placed vertically in the ground, with about 18in below the surface, and stand approximately 3ft×3ft above. Adjacent stones butt together and form an excellent boundary.

Stone walls always look well when built of the local material; they are works of skill and a pleasing feature of the landscape.

A typical dry stone wall on Lewis, Outer Hebrides, skilfully balanced with gaps between stones

6 Straw and Heather

Basket Making

Baskets have always fulfilled a variety of needs. For carrying fish, they had to be strongly built; these were made of osier or willow and came mostly from England, as did the oak lath spale baskets that are occasionally seen. Those locally made were fashioned out of oat straw, though the dried stems of dock plants were used to make 'dockens', a type of basket now to be seen in the museum at Lerwick. A docken was made of stalks about 2ft long, set vertically to form an open framework that was bound together with bents or marram grass.

The oat straw used in the making of Orkney baskets is normally the type called 'black oats', which gives the finished article a very attractive golden colour. These are still made by a few Orcadians, usually pensioners working on a part-time basis. A fair degree of proficiency in this craft can be acquired in about six months. The baskets are of all shapes and sizes; those known as 'cubbies' were used in the past for carrying peat, others are for general purposes and the basketwork is also featured in the backs of Orkney chairs.

The craftsman buys the straw in the sheaf, making certain that the stems are undamaged. It is then prepared by cleaning off the outside sheath, called a 'flag', and this takes quite a time. The other requirements are the needle and binding twine. In the past the twine would have been of bent or marram grass, which grows about 2ft high and can be twisted into a good binding. Today sisal is used.

When making a basket, the craftsman takes a handful of straw and binds it round with twine. This process continues in a circular fashion, with more straw being fed in and bound tightly by the twine, which is threaded through the layer to keep the work firm and compact as the basket is built up. The amount of straw used depends on the final thickness of the basketwork — a diameter of 1in is needed for a strong chair-back, but for baskets ½in is adequate. The craftsman can vary the diameter according to the size of basket required. It is part of his skill to give the article a pleasant curve outwards, narrowing again towards the top and ending with the topmost circle of straw completely bound with twine. The finished product is surprisingly strong and rigid. The procedure takes time, however, so the few baskets now being made are not cheap to buy.

In Shetland similar baskets are made, but on a lesser scale. The work is rather like that known as 'lipwork' done by gypsies and some old countrymen in England.

Rope Making

In the past crofters made much of their own rope for a variety of purposes from the materials at hand. Again straw came in useful, the rope being simply contrived by means of a straw twister — examples of which can be seen in many museums. More durable were ropes made from heather, as used to hold down roofs of heather-thatched crofts. The strongest and most long-lasting rope was of horse hair. On St Kilda the young men were lowered over the cliffs by horse-hair rope to collect birds and eggs for food. They had to make one of these ropes before they married.

An Orkney basket being woven from oat straw by Peter Foulis, of Kirkwall. Thick rings of straw tightly bound with twine are continuously built up to make a sturdy basket

Thatching

The traditional roof covering for crofts and farmbuildings was thatch. It could be put up anywhere and its comparative lightness avoided the need for heavy roof trusses and rafters — an important consideration owing to the scarcity of timber, particularly in the outlying islands. Alternatively, Ballachulish slates were used in some coastal areas where these could be brought in by sea, and stone slabs or tiles were common in Caithness.

Today thatch is still to be seen in the Uists and on Lewis; here and there in the Shetlands, but less often in the Orkneys, except on the surrounding isles. On the mainland, a mere handful of crofts are thatched, and these mostly in Caithness. Thatch is more commonly used on cow byres.

Before thatching begins, a foundation of turves has first to be laid on the roof. These measure 2ft by 1ft and are 2in thick. They are cut by a special spade with a curved blade so that each turf is slightly thicker in the middle. After being laid out to dry, the turves are hung in position on wooden pegs, overlapping in the same way as slates, and giving the roof layer a thickness of nearly 6in.

The thatch covering could be of different materials, with styles varying from one locality to another. Heather, laid about 1ft thick, gives a tough and durable cover. The best examples can be seen in the croft museums at Culloden, Glencoe and Auchindrain, in Argyll. Heather thatch is a rare sight on an occupied croft today, though it sometimes remains under a covering of straw, particularly in the Uists.

Oat straw is by far the most commonly used material. It is readily available and the thatch can be renewed yearly, certainly every other year. A windless day is essential for this task, otherwise the straw will be blown about. It is simply laid on the turves and covered by some old fishing net to hold it in place. The entire roof is then roped over, the ropes being 'anchored' by heavy stones suspended just below the eaves. These ropes, formerly of heather, later of sisal or hemp, are nowadays likely to be of nylon.

On this house in Uist the thatch is held in place with ropes anchored by heavy stones suspended beneath the eaves

A thatched croft at Boddam, Shetlands, with a grain dryer on the left

This thatched roof in Lewis, Outer Hebrides, is held down by ropes and netting weighted with heavy stones

In the Orkneys wild iris and reed are sometimes used in addition to oat straw. Another variation is for flat stone slabs to be laid along the roof edge to throw the rainwater clear of the walls. Generous overhangs are not practical as the high winds would get underneath and cause trouble. Penetration of water is the curse of all thatch covering: it rots the straw, damages the turves and eventually leads to the collapse of the roof.

In Lewis, as described in chapter 1, the thatched roofs of the black houses slope down to the sand-filled centre of the thick walls and through this the water escapes. Whether or not this made the houses damp is not known, but this kind of construction was prevalent at one time. These black houses and also the cow byres have rounded ends where the thatch is kept in position by ropes attached to a post; this pole runs from one extremity of the house to the apex of the roof, each end protruding at an angle of 45°.

These various types of roof covering with oat straw, heather and turves may be seen in the old crofts which have been restored to their original condition and are kept as museums.

7 Hide and Horn

Saddlery

With the virtual disappearance of working horses on farms over the past sixty years, saddlers and harnessmakers had a very thin time, but a few are still in business. In the Highlands, there are three who are overloaded with work and have orders for months ahead. Riding for pleasure and pony trekking are more popular than ever, with saddles and harness in constant demand, while special saddles for transporting deer carcases in the stalking season are also needed.

A saddle will last about seventy years if well looked after, but it requires a good deal of maintenance during its long life. Repairs include restuffing with wool flock, and renewing any parts that become worn or damaged, as well as restitching from time to time. Only the very best leather is used and practically all stitching is done by hand.

Donald Wright, whose shop in Huntly proudly displays the royal warrant, has two apprentices to help with his repair work; there was even a side-saddle awaiting his attention, and some new saddles are made there. Willie Munroe, of Beauly, is no longer young and has no apprentice to learn the trade. His speciality are the large, robust, long-lasting deer saddles. About forty of these were in his workshop awaiting repair before the start of the shooting season.

The third practising saddler, Charles Middleton, of Turriff, is probably the only one left in Scotland who concentrates on making harness. He turns out beautiful patent-leather collars for show purposes, as well as large peaked collars worn by Clydesdales in Glasgow. He too is snowed under with repair work on saddles and also makes new ones. It is a pity there are no apprentices; as with most saddlers, he appears to prefer to work on his own without distraction and without having to pay the high wages that young employees can command today. In the years to come, as the older men retire, there will be an acute shortage of qualified workers in leather to meet the demand.

These saddlers serve a wide area of the Highlands and have

Willie Munroe, of Beauly, specialises in making this type of heavy deer saddle used on ponies to transport the kill in the stalking season

Harness maker Charles Middleton, of Turriff, with a fine patent-leather horse-collar; in the background, an array of the tools of his trade

acquired a good reputation. There are also shops where saddlery is on sale, but without a saddler in practice.

Sheepskins

Sheepskins, as used widely for rugs and car-seat covers, and made up into garments and slippers, are very often the product of individuals who make a speciality of preparing them for sale. The Reawick Shetland Lamb Marketing Company, however, operates on a larger scale, as sheep are now being slaughtered in the Shetlands — formerly they were shipped live to the mainland — and consequently plenty of skins are available.

The sheepskins can be preserved quite easily until they are needed for processing. They can be kept in a refrigerator, or soaked in a solution of alum, and will keep for about a year if treated with about 2lb of salt and then rolled up.

When being prepared, any pieces of flesh are removed and the skin is washed in soapy water or detergent. It is then strung out tight on a wooden frame; when dry, the skin is brushed with a chrome solution and again left to dry. This process can be repeated and takes two or three days. When the skin is removed from the frame, the underside has a blue tinge from the colour of the chrome.

At this stage the sheepskin is rather stiff and rough, so it is held against an abrasive wheel which gives it a soft, pliable and smooth finish. The wool is then trimmed and combed ready for sale. While the majority of sheepskins are white or cream, some black and brown ones are often obtainable in the shops.

Deerskins

There is no shortage of deerskins, many of which are used for making suede; this is a specialised process needing machinery to split the skin. Some skins are prepared in the same way as sheepskins for use mostly as floor coverings, but they are less in demand. The hairs are rather brittle and naturally lack the warm, soft texture of sheep wool. Another drawback is that the deer will have been shot. Most experts will shoot a deer in the head to avoid damage to the hide, but others may aim at the heart or left shoulder where a bullet hole will detract from the value. Sometimes it is possible for a craftsman to select a flawless skin, but this is not always practicable.

Hornwork

There are more than a quarter of a million red deer in Scotland and they roam all over the Highlands. The stags grow magnificent antlers which are cast every spring and a new set is grown.

A sheepskin being dried at full stretch on a frame by Colin Plant, in the Orkneys

A considerable quantity of antlers are found by chance each year, usually by gillies who look after the big estates. A certain number of stags are also culled and shot, so that a good supply of antlers becomes available annually and these are used to make a variety of articles.

Antlers consist of a pair of main beams and from these grow the points — the number varies, with a royal head having 12. Considerable ingenuity is employed to obtain the maximum amount of items from the horn. In the centre is the pith or marrow going up towards the points, which are solid horn for the top two inches. The points are mostly made into cutlery handles, the tang being fixed into place with a resin glue.

Another small industry is the making of buttons, which are indestructible. Discs of horn are cut out by machine, the stitch holes are recessed and smoothed, and a light coat of wax is applied. The biggest producer of these staghorn buttons is the Kyleside Weavers and Handcraft company, of Bonar Bridge, whose output of over 50,000 is mostly achieved by workers in their own homes. These are reputed to be the best and a set was presented to the Queen on her Silver Jubilee.

The other big Highland concern in this field is McLean of Braemar, who has as little wastage as possible in the making of knife handles, buttons, medallions, toggle rings and so on. Staghorn polishes up well and should not be varnished.

Shepherd's Crooks

The carved crooks and horn-handled walking sticks seen in many of the craft shops are often made as a sideline by game-keepers and handymen. One of the best-known crook makers is Allister Campbell, of Loch Don on the Isle of Mull, who has built up his reputation over many years and has supplied samples of his craft to royalty.

The ram's horn of the Blackface sheep is the best working material for the crook part. It grows twisted like a short cork-screw and has first to be straightened and then curved to the required shape. The horn is cut in half, with the tip and some of the lower part removed. It is then boiled or heated with a burner to make it pliable, put into a vice and shaped. The hardened horn is fashioned with a rasp, the filing later becoming less abrasive as the work proceeds and is finally smoothed with sandpaper or crocus paper, or possibly boned to give a perfect finish. The carving or fancy work may take the form of a device such as a salmon or a thistle. The time spent on this fine carving will have a bearing on the price of the completed product.

A hole is then bored in the horn to take the shaft of the crook. Hazel is the most commonly used wood for this. It needs to be perfectly straight; sometimes it grows as required, but slight deviations can be corrected either by tying it to a 'splint' while it seasons or by steaming and straightening it. The top is then shaved to fit the hole, and a ferrule fixed to the bottom end. The shaft and horn are finished off with a coating — several, if necessary — of polyurethene.

The walking sticks are made in the same way. Sometimes the handles may be of deer antler, but this cannot be bent like ram's horn, and they are not so picturesque.

8 Wool

The quality, length and thickness of the wool used in local crafts varies with the breed of sheep. On the better pastures the Cheviot predominates, while on less good ground and in windy conditions the Blackface is most common. On the poorer uplands in the Shetlands, feeding largely on heather and able to exist where nothing else can survive, Shetland sheep are kept. This breed has very fine wool but not a very great weight of it as the animal is on the small side. It produces about 3lb of wool annually and, when crossed with another breed, about 5lb — even more if the pasture is good. A curious dietary feature is that Shetland sheep, and the ponies as well, enjoy eating seaweed that is exposed at low tide. The sheep on North Ronaldsay, in the Orkneys, live on seaweed alone, a high wall confining them to the foreshore.

The term 'Shetland wool' is one that is grossly abused. The Islands cannot produce anything like the quantity widely sold under the name; as one wool broker said, 'I doubt if it contains one per cent of Shetland wool.' The wool is comparatively short and not too easy to spin on its own, so longer stapled wool has to be added.

Elsewhere in the Islands the sheep are mostly Blackface and their wool is more suitable for making carpets. It was from Blackface wool that Harris tweed was originally made, with its characteristic rough look; this now comes in lighter weights of

Mrs Alex MacDonald of Drinishader, Harris, spinning wool

more sophisticated and fancier patterns, and the wool is obtained from any breed of sheep.

Brokers buy practically all the wool and sell it to the Wool Marketing Board on the mainland. The amount required in the Islands is returned dyed and made into yarn.

Milling

Hardly anybody today spins and dyes his own wool, though there has been a trend towards doing so as a pleasurable occupation, and also to making one's own garments, but little of this homespun produce ever reaches the market.

Many knitters in the area obtain their supplies from Hunters of Brora, a famous mill which processes the wool and weaves it. All wool has to be bought from a broker, and the sorting and grading is specialised work. Wool varies in quality and length depending on the part of the animal it comes from, the breed of sheep, the pasture, whether a ewe or a ram — a barren ewe, for instance, has a better fleece than one that has had twins. Then there is the colour, particularly of the native Shetland sheep which can be black, white or 'moorit' — brown.

The fleece is first scoured to remove dirt and oil, then the oil is put back. The wool is carded to get the fibres running the same way and to make the thread even; it is then spun. At some stage it is dyed: either before carding or afterwards in the hank. Later several yarns are spun together, to make two- or three-ply as required, and wound on to cones. Hand-frame knitters and weavers like their wool left on cones, while hand knitters prefer it by the hank.

Weaving

No weaving of any consequence is done in the crofts on the mainland, but a number of artist craftsmen have their own handlooms and run a good business, specialising in their own woven designs and making relatively short lengths of material

The tweed being woven on a hand loom by Miss Campbell of Drinishader

A Hattersley loom operated by John MacGregor, of Garenin, Lewis, to weave Harris tweed

to keep the patterns exclusive. In general, they aim at the top end of the market and in most cases their charges are very reasonable. If the business is small, it is best for them to own a shop and sell their own products. This saves commission to the middlemen and avoids the trouble of packing; also the weaver receives his money at once when he sells a piece. He can establish his business by building up a reputation over the years. On the other hand, customers will interrupt his work, particularly in the tourist season when the visitors are always fascinated to watch a weaver at his loom.

A variety of looms are used. Some craftsmen favour the old type of wooden loom; others prefer a Hattersley loom similar to the kind used for weaving Harris tweed. A power-driven loom is forbidden in the Hebrides if the cloth is to bear the orb mark of Harris tweed. When weavers have a surplus to sell, it can occasionally be bought in a craft shop. Besides the tweeds, many weavers produce hand-woven ties and shawls. The woven material is nearly always sent to a mill for finishing, as the facilities are so much better for washing, shrinking, milling or fulling, and pressing.

In general the type of person who sets up as a weaver does so because of his interest in the work, possibly his flair for design and the quality of his wool. In hand-weaving, everything must be of the best and that is why the majority of these craftsmen are successful.

Harris Tweed

According to the legal definition: 'Harris tweed must be made from 100-per-cent pure virgin wool produced in Scotland, then dyed, spun and finished in the Outer Hebrides and hand woven by the islanders at their own homes in the islands of Lewis, Harris, Uist, Barra and their several purtenances.' Tweed woven in accordance with these conditions, if in all ways satisfactory, is marked at its edge every three yards with the orb mark. The important factors are that the cloth should be woven in the crofters' homes and must be done by hand; although the wool has to be dyed, spun and finished in the Outer Hebrides, these operations need not necessarily be done by hand.

Originally Harris tweed was all woven in Harris, the mountainous southern end of the island that is attached to Lewis, and towards the end of the last century it had begun to gain a reputation in London. Lewis then began to produce cloth and during the early 1900s started to outstrip Harris. In 1909 the Harris Tweed Association was formed and the orb mark was registered and stamped on the tweed. As the years went by, an increasing amount of the wool was processed in factories, not all in the Hebrides. In 1934 a new definition for Harris tweed was produced, allowing the crofters to weave yarn that had been spun by the island's manufacturing companies. Over the years irregularities again began to creep in, and in 1964 judgment in court was made re-affirming the legal description of Harris tweed.

Hattersley looms are now used almost exclusively; while perhaps half a dozen or so of the old type of wooden hand looms are still in operation. It is interesting to note that two of the most distinguished users of the hand loom are women — weaving usually being considered a man's job, with spinsters doing the spinning and dyeing. Mrs Alex MacDonald and Miss Campbell, of Drinishader, to the south of Tarbert in Harris — where a notice proudly records that it was here that her Majesty the Queen was presented with a length of tweed in 1956 — have been weaving all their lives. Mrs MacDonald regularly gives demonstrations at the Royal Highland Show.

They do a certain amount of dyeing, using heather, water lily, bog myrtle and lichens to obtain the desired colour. The newly sheared whole fleece is put in a cauldron and boiled up with the selected dye; afterwards it is sent away for carding. Both weavers like to use hand-spun yarn for the weft and this they spin on their spinning wheels, which is a comparatively lengthy business. A hand-spun weft makes the cloth heavier, woollier and warmer.

The fleeces are returned from the mill ready spun for making the warp. It takes about two hours to set up the loom. When this has been done, approximately a yard of cloth can be woven each hour, though the amount depends on the intricacy of the pattern and the thickness of the wool. Variations are made by raising and lowering the heddles by means of foot pedals. Yarn of different colours is put in the shuttles, four of which can be used. A lot of work remains to be done after the weaving.

Miss Campbell weaves only short lengths of tweed, 10 yards at a time, so that it can be washed easily. It is first tramped in a wooden tub then banged on a board, the hardest physical part of the work. This is the fulling process that partially felts the tweed and makes it nicer to handle, at the same time shrinking its width from 32in to 28in. Finally it is sent away to be stamped with the orb. Both weavers sell their tweed themselves, not through a wholesaler, and have built up such a reputation over the years that they cannot catch up with demand.

Apart from these isolated cases where old methods are used, the remaining weavers work with Hattersley domestic looms that are semi-automatic, the motive power being supplied by the feet working pedals attached to a cranked driving shaft. These looms were widely adopted in the mid-1920s when Lord Leverhulme was making strenuous efforts to revitalise and modernise industry in the Hebrides. Over the years around 1,200 have been supplied, about half of which are probably still in use. These machines, substantially built of metal, are both ingenious and simple. They are operated almost exclusively by men, as it is comparatively heavy and tiring work. In practice a number of the weavers are crofters; their farming activities take up most of their working hours in the summer, particularly at harvest time, so the tendency is to weave in the winter evenings. Virtually all the weaving is now done in Lewis, a mere handful of weavers operating in Harris and Uist.

At its peak, production reached seven million yards of single-width cloth a year; around 70 per cent of this was exported, mostly to the USA. The wool used in making the cloth does not necessarily come from the Hebrides, where the sheep are mostly Blackface on the poorer pastures and Cheviot crosses on the better ground. Only about a third of their own requirements are produced and this is supplemented by wool from the mainland. Wherever it is produced, the wool for Harris tweed has to be spun and dyed in the Hebrides. In addition it is scoured, carded, blended and hand warped. The factories' designers produce up-to-date patterns, gay in colour and attractive to look at. The tweed is in different weights, suitable for women's wear and furnishing material, as well as the heavier traditional men's suitings. No longer is the yarn made up of individual colours. A single yarn sometimes consists of ten different shades to achieve the right effect.

The looms have four heddles and up to six shuttles, which are operated automatically by cams on the driving shaft, so the permutations in the woven pattern are innumerable. As an added refinement the machine has a self-tensioning device. The wool is still hand warped in the factory where the basic pattern of the colours is prepared by winding the threads on to a frame of wooden pegs, taking care to keep the tension even throughout. The warp is then gathered together in hanks and sent to the weaver with the wool for the weft and exact instructions about the pattern.

On receipt, the weaver has to set up the warp; this entails threading 648 threads and takes several hours. It will weave a cloth 32in wide, later to be shrunk a little at the factory. Occasionally a thread breaks and has to be joined with a knot, which is dealt with by the factory at a later stage. The completed piece of cloth, approximately 85 yards in length, is sent to the factory for finishing; there it is held up against the light and critically examined by women who undo the knots and invisibly mend any faults. If necessary, the cloth can be cropped to remove the hairy look, though this is a feature of rougher garments. A final inspection on a long table is given to ensure it is perfect. Lastly it is marked with the orb sign by an official of the Harris Tweed Association before being baled for dispatch. In spite of high production the industry is slowly declining; because it is a top-quality cloth and can never be cheap, the effects of economic recession have been noticeably strong.

Occasionally a weaver markets his own tweed, by means of a mail order service or by opening a shop in a tourist area. There are several at work in Harris and Uist. In this case, the yarn is probably bought from the factory, and the finishing will also be done there. An economical way is for the weaver to purchase remainders of yarn, such as the ends of batches of a particular dye, and design his own pattern.

A controversy about the width of the cloth came to a head in 1976. Manufacturers of suits are geared to dealing with double-width cloth and computer-controlled cutting. The Hattersley looms produce only single-width cloth. The proposal put to the weavers was that they should make double-width cloth on power looms in small factories scattered about the Islands. This would bring the industry up to date, but the part-time weavers would lose their independence and it would be difficult for them to undertake short stints of weaving. A vote was taken and the crofters decided by 497 to 55 against a change in the present arrangements.

This gave an indication of the number of weavers at work — some 550 compared with more than twice as many five years ago. Those still operating tend to be the hard core who have stepped up their production, and it looks as if another 600 looms are lying idle. The loom is the property of the weaver; it will cost around £1,200 today, about a third of this subsidised by the Highlands and Islands Board.

The industry is going through an uneasy phase, and the final outcome is of great consequence to the livelihood of the Islanders.

On Fair Isle — a name world famous for its hand-knitted sweaters — Mrs Thompson displays one of traditional design

Knitting

Knitting has always been an important home industry in the Islands as there was little alternative work for the women. They would spin the wool, turn it into knitting yarn and colour it with vegetable dye. They knitted sweaters for the menfolk, who were nearly all fishermen, and for the children — a best one for Sundays, another for school and a third for working. Knitted garments were also traded for groceries or taken by fishing boat and sold on the mainland.

The most famous of all is the Fair Isle knitting, possibly originating from designs from a wrecked galleon of the Spanish Armada or perhaps influenced by Scandinavian tradition. The name and style of Fair Isle knitting has spread far afield, but on the island itself only a very small proportion is produced, the total population being about seventy, including men and children. A hundred years ago nearly 400 people were living in great hardship on Fair Isle and to relieve distress a large number were settled in Nova Scotia.

The Fair Isle patterns are sometimes picked out in natural colours of undyed wool, ranging from white to grey, black and moorit — a brown colour which is the most prized of all. Alternatively the wool was dyed; examples of the brilliant colours are to be seen in the museum at Lerwick.

Knitting is expanding into a sizeable industry. When the time taken to hand-knit a garment is assessed and added to the cost of the wool, the realistic price that should be charged for it is far too high to make it readily saleable. Most garments are therefore partly, if not wholly, made on hand-frame knitting machines. Jerseys, for instance, are usually knitted by machine, except for the patterned yokes which are hand-knitted. The machines cost about £200 upwards and are so elaborate that really excellent work can be produced on them at a greatly increased speed.

An expert knitter of the Sanday Island co-operative working to a specified design for sale to exclusive shops abroad

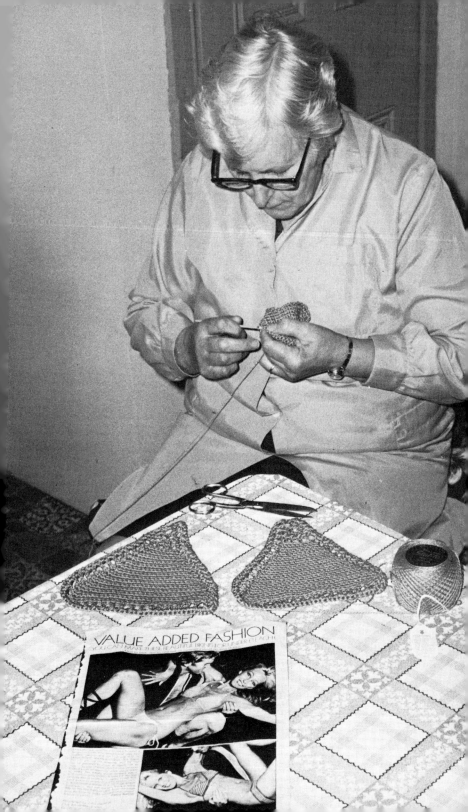

VALUE ADDED FASHION

The knitters undertake this work partly because they enjoy it and partly to make some pocket money. The great advantage is that they work at home and in their own time. Each knitter is paid for her output, so she can please herself how hard she works. They often undercharge for the hours they put in and few of them knit full-time for a living. The shops find it difficult to obtain enough of these home-knitted goods which, relatively low priced and of attractive design, are an extremely good buy.

Knitting is becoming a better organised activity, particularly in the Islands where production scarcely meets the demand. It is outstandingly well run in the little island of Sanday, in the Orkneys, where a hundred knitters work in a co-operative, selling to exclusive shops all over the world, in particular to America. These knitters work to a high standard, producing garments of a specified design and using special, carefully chosen wool. The finished articles are minutely inspected and attractively packed. The knitters, who all live in crofts, are paid a fair price so that they can earn a living. Many of them are young and use the proceeds to improve their crofts, often buying a deep freeze. It is an arrangement that keeps everyone happy.

Shetland Shawls

Shetland shawls are famous throughout the world for the excellence of the knitting and the extremely fine quality of the wool which comes from the pure-bred Shetland sheep. In early summer a sheep casts or moults its winter coat which remains on its back as a mat of wool and begins to rise or lift. At this stage it can be removed by 'rooing' or plucking — that is, pulling it off in a complete fleece — a process that takes about five minutes. A few individual sheep may still be rooed, as was the practice in earlier times, but the majority are hand sheared. Each gives some 3lb of wool, bringing in about £1. Any sheep

Mrs Monat and Mrs Priest, two sisters who specialise in knitting Shetland shawls passing one through a wedding ring.

that elude the round-up at shearing time will moult their wool up on the pasture. This used to be collected in special wool-gathering baskets, which are now museum pieces.

The next operation is to card and spin the wool: this is done while in its greasy state. A pair of shaped platters, whose faces are composed of wire brushes, were used to brush the wool, a small piece at a time. In this carding process much of the dirt falls out and the wool is formed into a fluffy rolag, ready for spinning. Every croft had its spinning wheel which the spinsters worked. This was usually the vertical kind that takes up little space. Until recently, when they attracted the attention of antique buyers, these spinning wheels could be obtained quite easily, but have now become scarce. Most of them are very old, having been handed down over many years.

These methods of carding and spinning were slow and laborious. Nobody in Shetland does them by hand nowadays, except as a soothing pastime. As with the other Islands, all the wool goes to the mainland mills for carding, spinning, washing and turning into yarn. About half the wool from Shetland is returned to the islanders for knitting.

The world-famous shawls — the Shetland knitters' highest achievement — are today produced on a very small scale, almost entirely in the northernmost island of Unst. The best quality shawl is of single-ply, hand-spun wool so fine that — although it measures $1\frac{3}{4}$yd square — it can be passed through a wedding ring. These are still made on Unst by three dedicated knitters, the most famous being Mrs Monat and Mrs Priest, two sisters who recently won first prize at the Royal Highland Show for a shawl and a stole. They are no longer young and such is the fineness of the wool that their output is necessarily small. Each item is a collector's piece almost too good to use.

The shawls are always white and knitted in traditional patterns. The knitting is done with two needles, the end of one being securely fixed in a hole in a pad attached to a belt worn around the waist. The work commences with the lace edge at the bottom, goes on to the bottom border and progresses up

The web-like delicacy of a Shetland shawl

through the centre to the top. The three remaining borders are then worked and finally the rest of the lace edging; all are knitted together so that the joins do not show. This may take months and frequently the two sisters combine to finish the work. The very few orders they accept are made only by personal contact and for the completed work that will have occupied them for hundreds of hours they ask a mere pittance. In common with many other craftsmen they think that nobody would buy their wares if they charged a realistic price.

There is no reason why others could not take up this type of knitting, though with the present tempo of living few young people have the patience or inclination for such work. It requires great concentration and accuracy, and while it is possible to knit and talk, it is not possible to watch television at the same time. It is sincerely hoped that this attractive craft will not be allowed to die out.

Kilt Making

The Scottish kilt has evolved over the years from a length of woollen cloth, woven in colours obtained from vegetable dyes, to a carefully made garment mostly of tartan design. Kilts are made in great numbers, being widely worn in Scotland and by Scotsmen all over the world. Several hundred distinct tartans are specially woven, and the design varies according to each clan.

'Tartan' is derived from the French word denoting a kind of woollen material. It was mentioned in the royal accounts of James V, father of Mary Queen of Scots, as long ago as 1538. Following the Battle of Culloden in 1746 the wearing of tartan in any form was banned, except by the Highland regiments. This restriction remained in force for thirty-six years, until the act was repealed in 1782. The kilt was given a new lease of life in 1822 when George IV wore one on a visit to Edinburgh — with pink tights underneath. At a later date Balmoral was to become a favourite residence of Queen Victoria and a special Balmoral tartan was designed by the Prince Consort.

The method of making kilts has now been standardised. Each takes no less than 8 yards of material. Great care and skill is needed to measure out the pleats so that the overall pattern remains symmetrical. Each of the twenty-seven to thirty pleats must be exactly similar — a matter of particular significance on military occasions. The stitching is done by hand on the inside of the pleats; the women who do this work take one to two days for each kilt.

Three measurements are taken when fitting a kilt: waist, hips and length. The garment has no hem and, once completed, the length cannot be adjusted.

Kilts are also made up in plain tweeds, as worn by certain Irish regiments with distinguishing emblems at the side. Regimental kilts are lined with flannel across the small of the back; this makes them extremely warm, as many a Highland soldier

Kilt making: this 8-yard length of material goes to make one kilt

has found to his cost when serving in hot climates, but they are ideal in his native land.

A good kilt is expensive, costing £100 or more. But bearing in mind the quality and quantity of the cloth, the skill required in making it up, and the fact that it is very long lasting — as well as having great panache — any Scotsman considers it money well spent.

9 Coopering

Whisky Barrels

The barrels in which whisky is matured are supplied by the coopering industry. It is a curious fact that the barrels, always of oak, are made from second-hand timber — that is, wood in the form of 100-gallon sherry butts or dismantled American bourbon barrels.

Sherry butts are becoming scarcer now that increasing use is being made of containers, and cost around £80 each. Each weighs half a ton when full, so it must be handled with care to avoid damage. Owing to age or rough handling, the staves have to be renewed from time to time; the replacements are obtained from other barrels that have been dismantled when past repair.

Fitting new staves is a skilled and exact science. The sherry butt is set upright with the bottom lid removed. The hoops are taken off, with the exception of the top one holding the staves in position, and a trussing hoop is slipped over the barrel. With some difficulty the broken staves are taken out and the replacements inserted. The last to be put in must be an exact fit to keep the barrel watertight. This is done by a combination of measurement and eye. The stave is planed down on a machine to obtain the correct width, with a slight angle along its side to allow for the radius of the barrel. The hoops are then replaced, and the bottom end re-fitted and made watertight by caulking it with a rush — the common bulrush is used for this purpose.

The American bourbon barrels pose different problems. Originally made to hold 40 gallons, they have to be remade into

dump hogsheads to contain about 55 gallons. As they are not permitted to be used more than once or twice in the United States, the dismantled sections, which arrive tied in bundles, are in comparatively good condition. They have been charred on the inside to neutralise the bourbon and sterilise them — a process that does not impair the whisky.

In practice about five of the dismantled barrels will make up into four larger-sized ones for maturing whisky. The cooper takes a new top hoop and a bundle of staves and proceeds to fit the staves round the hoop to form the barrel; this takes considerable dexterity and unless great care is exercised the structure collapses like a pack of cards. Special trussing hoops are then forced over the barrel to hold it rigid. A rim has to be cut inside the top to take the lid; a tool called a croze is used for this. As the barrel has been enlarged, the original lid is too small; a new panel must be inserted and completely reshaped to the new size. The barrels are steamed to make the wood pliable and the six hoops are forced on as tightly as possible, either by hammering or on a machine.

The hoops, with a slight bevel to fit the sloping sides of the barrel, are made by the cooper and riveted up to the exact size required. The only opening is the bung hole in the top through which it is filled. Finally comes the pressure testing with air and water to ensure watertightness before the barrel is despatched to the distillery.

Whisky will mature only in barrels, not in bottles. By law it cannot be sold until it is at least three years old. The Highland malt whiskies are frequently very much older as most of them improve with age. The maturing process can take up to twenty years — indeed Grant's Jubilee Malt Whisky is twenty-five years old.

With the long maturing period there is a slow turnover of barrels which are mostly ready for re-use as soon as emptied.

Raising a whisky barrel from the dismantled sections of an American bourbon barrel

They are returned to the cooper only when repairs are needed and might well have a life of twenty or thirty years. Thus the cooper spends half his time repairing barrels and half in making new ones, either as replacements or for use in expansion of the distillery. The proportion varies according to requirements; business was slack around 1974 and most of the work was repairing, but it is picking up again and more new barrels are being made.

Every distillery employs an experienced cooper to supervise and inspect the barrels. When repairs are needed they are sent away to one of the coopering firms.

The craft of coopering is an essential one as long as there is whisky to be matured, so its future is assured. There is a steady entry of apprentices into the trade, despite the lure of high pay for any jobs connected with the oil industry. They receive a reasonably good wage, though in this very skilled craft they do not pay their way for two or three years. The apprenticeship lasts four years, having been recently reduced from five.

Coopers are paid piecework and work extremely hard at their job, which requires much physical energy, speed and precision.

In the north the coopering industry is centred round Dufftown, Craigellachie and Aberdeen, in close proximity to the famous malt distilleries in the area.

Fish Barrels

Traditionally the containers needed for salted herrings and sprats were made of wood, but plastic ones are being used on an increasing scale. These are more readily obtainable, a little cheaper and do not leak — an important factor when carried in refrigerated ships.

One cooper is at work full-time making fish barrels at Wick, and another makes them in the winter in the Shetlands; their products are supplemented by barrels made abroad.

Unlike those for whisky and beer, barrels for fish are made of spruce, which arrives at the cooperage in ready-cut bundles.

Fish barrels are used for the export of salted herring

The staves are given a taper at each end by a circular saw into which they are fed on a curve to produce the desired effect. The barrel is then formed into shape using only the top hoop to hold the staves in position. Whereas most coopers steam the barrels to make the staves pliable for trussing and gathering, at Wick they are shaped by the age-old method of damping them and placing them over a fire burning offcuts and shavings. After about five minutes the wood becomes quite pliable and hoops can be forced down the barrel, drawing together the staves at the bottom end.

The barrel is then put on a machine, held in a horizontal

position and revolved, while a plucker plane hung on a piece of rope planes the whole of the outside, the operation taking three or four minutes. Next a croze is used to cut a rim to take the lid, which nowadays is supplied ready made. Lids are fitted at either end, and six metal hoops are riveted and forced on. A small hole is drilled in the top, the cooper blows into this to see if it holds the pressure and the job is complete. Nine or ten barrels can be made in a day, a good deal of preparatory work being done beforehand.

Wick in its hey-day around 1911-13 had an output of $2\frac{1}{4}$ million barrels of herring, exported principally to Russia, Germany and Scandinavia. To cope with the demand, 500 coopers were employed. The drastic decline in the salt-fish industry has reduced the number of its full-time coopers in Scotland to a single individual.

10 Proceeds from the Sea

Drying Fish

In the Orkneys, Shetlands and Fair Isle, fish are dried in the summer months when there is a surplus and fishing conditions are good. They are first gutted and washed, then placed in a bucket of pickling salt for four or five days and afterwards hung out on a line to dry. This can take some time as the salt tends to absorb moisture, and wind and sunshine are needed to finish the process. Alternatively the fish are dried by hanging them over the kitchen range. They are mainly whiting, haddock and ling, though any kind of fish can be dried. Before being eaten they are usually skinned and some of the salt is removed by soaking and boiling.

Fish drying declined following the connection of the electricity supply to every croft. Any surplus fish are now put in the deep freeze and need little preparation. To many people it tastes better when preserved by freezing than by salting.

Salted Herrings

Production of salted herrings is carried on fairly extensively in Lerwick and Stornoway, though the decline in the number of fish has reduced output. Nearly all of it is exported, mostly to the USA, South Africa and the Scandinavian countries, where it is often eaten raw; in Britain, it would only be served in this state in hors d'oeuvres.

There used to be a huge trade in salted herrings in Scotland.

Drying fish on a line in Fair Isle
Salting herrings at Lerwick

It was a major industry in Wick, but has now almost ceased. For girls in the Shetlands gutting fish was about the only work available. They followed the fishing fleets around during the herring season, working in teams of three — two gutters and one packer — wearing leather boots and oilskin aprons.

The gutting is now done by machine; the heads are left on, otherwise the salted fish deteriorates down the spine. The herrings are put in large barrels of salt brine and left to cure for a fortnight. They are then removed and packed neatly and as tightly as possible into barrels with a large quantity of salt. The combination of the salt and the moisture from the fish produces the preserving brine. When a barrel has been fully packed with about 1,000 herrings, a cooper puts the lid on and forces a hoop down over the top. Each barrel is topped up with brine through a small hole in the head, a wooden spile peg is hammered in to make it watertight and it is ready for despatch.

For household consumption, herrings are packed in plastic buckets and sealed with a lid. Before cooking, the fish need soaking for twenty-four hours to remove the salt. Local people say that a salt herring is the best cure for a cold — a statement which should be taken literally 'with a pinch of salt' as a similar claim is made for whisky.

Kippers

Kippers are herrings that have been smoked, complete with bone and head, using oak sawdust. This is done when the herrings are at their best — from June to September they are in good condition, fat and oily. One producer who prides himself on the quality of his kippers is Sid Watson, of Kirkwall, who goes up to the Shetlands and waits till the fish are just right, testing them by feeling their condition in his hand. When satisfied, he buys his requirements and has them sent to Kirkwall, where they are put in a deep freezer for use as required. He affirms that the best herring come from the Stacks of Shetland.

The traditional smoking kiln consists of a brick-built chamber about 4 yards square, though the size may vary. The chamber narrows to form a chimney at the top about 1 yard square. The prepared herrings are fixed on tenterhooks on wooden bars — about sixteen fish to a bar — and hung in the chamber 3-4 ft above the floor. When the kiln is loaded, oak sawdust and possibly some wooden chips are placed in heaps on the floor and set alight. The smoke rises slowly, passes up through the fish and emerges from the chimney, spreading a pleasant aroma around the vicinity. From time to time more sawdust is added to keep the fires going, and the draught is carefully controlled by regulating the kiln doors.

Good oak sawdust is not very easy to obtain and one kipper producer from Stornoway in the Outer Hebrides sends a lorry to collect his supply from the cooperage works at Dufftown.

The normal practice is to light the fires in the evening and remove the herrings as kippers next morning, and smoke another lot during the day. A kipper gets its characteristic taste from the chemicals that rise up as smoke; over the years the sides of the kiln are turned jet black.

Part of the colour of a kipper is obtained from a vegetable dye which affects the appearance and does not alter the taste. The kippering process acts as a very slight preservative to the fish which must be eaten fresh.

The more modern way, which is quicker and more efficient, is to use a 'Torry' kiln in which the fumes from oak sawdust are circulated through the fish by a fan. However, the connoisseurs of a good kipper say they can tell the difference and prefer those produced by the old method.

Fish are hung on tenterhooks for smoking in this kiln at Stornoway

Smokies

Smokies — or smoked haddock — are a speciality of Arbroath, which is not in the Highlands, but some are made elsewhere, notably in Aberdeen. The method originated in Scandinavia.

Fresh haddock are gutted and their heads are cut off; then they are tied in pairs by their tails and strung on sticks. These are put in a smoking chamber heated by a fire of oak and beech wood, and the top is covered with a damp piece of sacking which keeps in most of the heat and smoke. Experience is needed to judge how long to leave them in the chamber; usually the process takes between thirty and ninety minutes. The smokies are by that time actually cooked, and should be eaten hot straight out of the smoking chamber to enjoy them at their best.

Finnan Haddock

Finnans were originally made at the tiny village of Findon, just to the south of Aberdeen, but their popularity has spread far afield. The process is similar to that used for kippers, the haddock being smoked, with all their bones, in 'London' kilns. The fish are given a short dip in brine, then placed in a smoking chamber and smoked for about twelve hours at a fairly high temperature. Plenty of sawdust, including some from softwood, is needed to generate enough heat. The heat gives the fish a dry texture, and the smoke its colour and some of the flavour. Finnans, which can be kept a long time, must be cooked before being eaten.

Other Smoked Fish

Smoked salmon is a great delicacy. The fish are gutted and filleted by hand, and smoked with a lot of heat; this preserves them and they keep for several months. Smoked salmon is eaten without further cooking.

Other fish that are smoked include mackerel, which require

a lot of heat, and whiting, which are lightly smoked. These are invariably filleted and soaked in brine, with vegetable colouring that gives them their yellow appearance.

Lobsters

High-powered boats enable lobster fishermen to cover a wide area farther offshore as nearby places become fished out; these are constructed with ample space in the stern to accommodate the creels. Lobster pots are no longer made in the traditional

Lobster creels at Stromness, Orkneys

way, using willow rods for the frame. A creel consists of a base-board, usually of wood, on which the bait is fixed, with some heavy stones to anchor it. Three or four cane rods are secured to this base and bent in the form of a semi-circle, the whole framework being covered with nylon netting. The ends have funnel-shaped openings which allow the lobster to enter but, once inside, it cannot get out. A new development is to use steel rods instead of cane; these are welded together to form a creel that is stronger and more durable, and this type is becoming more generally used.

When caught, the lobster has rubber rings placed round its claws so that it cannot open them — a lobster's muscles are weak for opening and very strong for closing. Lobsters are kept in large tanks and flown to the Continent when there is a load ready for despatch. Few remain to be eaten in Britain.

Crabs, too, are caught in creels; at one time they were thrown away, but now have a marketable value.

Seaweed

Seaweed is collected and used on a surprisingly large scale. In the Orkneys alone over 1,000 tons are harvested annually. Two kinds are collected — bladder weed and tangle; the latter, with a stem and long fronds, has good jelling qualities. In Uist, seaweed is eaten when made into carrageenan, a jelly-like pudding.

The weed is sometimes dried; it may also be left in large nets in the water to be hoisted aboard small ships, called puffers, which ply the area with all types of cargo.

In the Outer Hebrides, seaweed was used extensively to provide manure for making lazy beds for potatoes. Layers of seaweed were covered with earth and fertilised the beds that were made in wet and inhospitable soil. Traces of the beds are still to be seen, with a central ridge about 1ft high and 3ft across, and a shallow trough between each bed. The appearance is similar to the pattern left by the old ridge-and-furrow method of ploughing, though the beds are narrower.

Today a number of crofters supplement their earnings, and some even make a living, by collecting seaweed to supply the Alginate Industries in the Outer Hebrides. These factories dry the weed and turn it into dark-coloured granules which are sent to the main alginate factory at Barcaldine, north of Oban, for processing into a final form. It is used in an astonishing variety of ways as an ingredient of jellies, ice cream, paint and pharmaceuticals and by the textile industry. In fact, seaweed in one form or another is probably encountered daily by everyone.

11 Proceeds from the Land

Peat Digging

Peat covers ten per cent of Scotland and although it renders the ground useless it is still valued as a fuel. A lot of labour and time is needed to dig out and dry the peat, however, and older people are tending to use more convenient though expensive fuels. In Scotland it is not, as it is in Ireland, exploited for running power stations. Apart from domestic uses, it is burnt in the fires when malting barley, the pleasant aroma giving a subtle flavour to the malt that goes to make whisky.

Winning peat is hard work. It is possible to cut it mechanically but most of the ground is unfriendly and only the whisky firms can afford the necessary machinery. Crofters and householders are allocated peat banks or diggings, the lucky ones getting them close to the road. The top spit of the bank is first removed and a curious cutting tool with a deep blade, called a tushker — a name with regional variations — is used to dig out the peat. In Skye and some other places, a spade is preferred and serves the purpose just as well.

Peat is dug in May and laid out to dry; it is later placed upright so that the wind can continue the drying process and to let it develop a hard outer skin. In the autumn the peat is transported to the croft by tractor and trailer; in some more inaccessible part of the Shetlands sledges are still in use. It is stacked with air gaps between individual peats to allow the drying to go on, and used as required for cooking and heating.

In Fair Isle, where the peat has nearly all been worked out, oil is taking its place as a domestic fuel. In the Orkneys too it is becoming scarce and can only be obtained in the remoter parts. In Lewis 80 per cent of the island is covered in peat, the land west of Stornoway lying derelict under a blanket of it for miles. However, in some places the peat has been entirely removed and 10,000 acres of land on Lewis are now fertile.

Corn Milling

There are still a few mills in the Highlands where corn is ground with stones; one is at Sandhaven, in Aberdeenshire, and another, at John o'Groats, is operated by Magnus Houston whose family has owned it for over 200 years. These two mills run only part of the time as the millers are also crofters who are busy on their land in the summer months. Oats are milled at Sandhaven, and bere at John o'Groats. Bere, or bear, is a kind of barley that grows better in the very limy soil than some other crops. It is also grown in the Orkneys and Shetlands,

Peat being dug on Skye

Turves of peat neatly stacked ready for winter use in Uist

where the local people consider it the best ingredient for making porridge, scones and black puddings. It has a coarse outer shell and long awns, or spikes, which are removed by a machine called a hummeler.

The grain has first to be dried over a fire, then ground to remove the husks, riddled and sieved to free the dust and finally milled with a granite or French burr stone. Some 3 or 4 tons can be milled in a full working day. Stone-ground cereal is widely considered to be second to none.

The grinding stones need to be dressed two or three times a year, each pair taking a day. At both mills the millers themselves do the dressing — a process of cutting grooves in the stones by means of a mill bill and thrift, a chisel-shaped instrument with a sharp edge.

The wheels at the John o'Groats mill are driven by an overshot waterwheel, while at Sandhaven electric power is used, the mill wheel now being unserviceable.

Malting Barley

Malted barley is used to make whisky and beer. The traditional method is to steep the barley in water for two days and then spread it, to a depth of about 6in, over the malting floor where it remains for five days, being frequently ploughed through with special rakes to mix it up. During this time the barley heats up, germinates and starts to sprout; rootlets grow, causing the starch in the grain to turn sugary. With wooden or tin shovels,

A peat-burning fireplace in a Fair Isle house

The mill at John o' Groats where bere, a kind of barley, is stone ground

the barley is then loaded into a kiln where heat from a furnace below percolates up through the grains, making them hard and dry, with a pleasant malt taste if chewed.

When malting for whisky, the kiln is fired with peat, a faint aroma of which, some people claim, can be detected in the flavour of the liquor. A little heather is sometimes put in to burn with the peat as an added refinement.

After drying, the grains are sifted to remove the rootlets which, together with the husks, are made up into pellets for animal feed.

This old method of malting, by spreading the barley on the floor, is becoming obsolete, though some distilleries still use it. It served its purpose for many years, but needs careful management and even so the results vary slightly. The pagoda-shaped roof of the malting — the building where the barley is malted — can be seen in many a distillery complex; most distillers retain it as a decoration, whether or not they do their own malting.

In practice most of the malt is now supplied to the distilleries by specialist firms whose methods are more scientific and reliable. Greater attention is also paid to the growing of barley, and the north and east parts of Scotland are ideal for producing grain suitable for malting. Farmers sow their crops under contract to the malting firms who specify the type to be sown and advise which fertiliser to use. The harvested barley is brought straight to the maltings where it is scientifically dried in preparation for the process of malting to start.

The important feature of malted barley is the sugar content, which determines the alcoholic strength of the liquor. After water and yeast have been added at the distillery, the fermentation turns this sugar into alcohol, so more sugar means a higher

From these stills the renowned Glenlivet malt whisky is produced

strength of the spirit. The finished malt is therefore tested for sugar content and flavour before being despatched to the distilleries.

Whisky Distilling

There are two types of whisky: the 'malts' made from malted barley, and the 'grain' from maize, rye and oats. Grain whisky is easier and quicker to produce as it is made in a continuously operated still, whereas with malt whisky the 'wash' — the fermented liquid — has to be distilled twice. Most whisky is sold as a blended mixture of both types, though an increasing amount is marketed as 'single malt' — the unblended product of one distillery.

Whisky has been distilled in the Highlands for several hundred years. At one time most of it was done illicitly to avoid paying duty, and there was continual conflict with the excise men. When the situation eased, the distilleries gradually became legalised. The first licence was taken out in 1824 by 'the Glenlivet', the jealously guarded name of the most famous of all malt whiskies and regarded by many connoisseurs as the finest in the world.

Most of the malt whisky is produced in the Highlands, Islands and the Grampian region where the water — a vital ingredient in the process — is particularly suitable. Glenlivet obtain theirs from a well; others use peaty burn water. It is curious how whisky of slightly varying taste is produced by different distillers following the same methods.

Whisky distilling is a skilled craft, a pleasurable occupation — some would say a very necessary one. The malted barley is bruised and put into a large mash tin; hot water is added to form a pulp, called the 'wort', of several thousand gallons. This is fed into large stainless steel tanks, the yeast is added and allowed to ferment for several days.

It is then ready for distilling — that is, the alcohol is extracted by vapourising, then channelled off to a condenser and liquefied. Alcohol vapourises at a lower temperature than water.

The 'wash' is distilled first into a big copper wash still; and secondly into a slightly smaller, low wine still. The first vapour given off, called 'foreshots', is poisonous and kept separate from the rest of the liquid and later distilled again; the 'aftershots' are similarly treated. The procedure is carefully supervised by the stillman who observes the distilled spirit in a glass box called a 'safe'.

The final operation is to pour the raw whisky into barrels. It is quite colourless and undrinkable when first made, but it improves as it matures, and gets its golden colour from the wood of the barrel. As the barrels are filled, a customs officer is always in attendance; the amount is carefully measured and recorded, and the quantity and date painted on the barrel. It then goes to a bonded warehouse to mature for the statutory three years, though it is invariably kept much longer. As whisky matures at different rates in each distillery, on average it is allowed to mature for seven years. The barrels are slightly porous, leading to an evaporation loss of about 2 per cent a year — a distressing thought when it comes to Grant's 25-year-old Jubilee malt whisky.

The production cost is relatively low, about £2.50 a gallon, but the duty of almost £30 is what puts the price up. However, the industry has been expanding steadily, with a slight setback in 1974-5, and a great deal of whisky goes for export.

Cheese Making

During the summer months a certain amount of farmhouse cheese finds its way into the shops, mostly in the Orkneys. In Kirkwall, Scott's shop, which supplies it to Queen Elizabeth the Queen Mother, proudly displays the royal warrant.

The cheese is made only when the house cow produces more milk than is required by the crofter's family. Any surplus milk cannot be sold to the public as it is uneconomical for a small producer to install the equipment necessary to comply with the regulations.

This is how a farmer's wife makes the cheese. The milk, brought in fresh from milking, is neither pasteurised nor skimmed. To 8gal of milk add a spoonful of cheesemaking mixture, consisting mainly of rennet. Warm this in a pan on the stove for about 20 mins, to approximately blood heat. It then becomes solid. Break this up and add salt. The cheese will sink to the bottom. Remove the pan from the stove and leave it to settle. Pour the whey off the top (this is fed to the pigs). Leave it to strain in a muslin bag all night. Finally, put the contents into a cheese press lined with a muslin bag.

The press is a cylindrical-shaped canister with small holes in the side to let out surplus moisture. A lid is put on the top and pressure applied with a specially made spring, though a heavy weight would do equally well. This is left for half a day, then removed from the press and reversed, with pressure again applied for a short time. A 2lb cheese can then be taken out; three 2lb cheeses are made from 8gal of milk.

The cheese can be eaten immediately or kept for several months. During this time it will develop a thin skin and should be turned over daily so that it maintains its shape and does not split. It is a matter of personal preference as to when it is eaten.

Home-made cheese being pressed by Mrs Hepburn in the Orkneys

12 Sporting Equipment

Fishing Rods

The opportunities for fishing in the Highlands and Islands are outstanding, and as this sporting activity has more participants than any other there is a big demand for rods. These were formerly made of greenheart wood, but this became very difficult to obtain and an alternative had to be found. Three different materials are now used: split cane, glass-fibre and carbon fibre.

The majority of fishermen use glass-fibre rods which can be produced by factory methods and are the cheapest at around £40, while split cane costs £100 and carbon fibre £130. After some teething troubles, carbon fibre may prove to be as good as any — it is also being tried out for golf clubs with promising results.

The split-cane rods favoured by a great many fishermen are carefully built by craftsmen with the aid of some machinery, though the process cannot be mechanised to any great extent. For nearly 100 years split-cane rods have been made from bamboo imported from China; it arrives in 9ft lengths of 3in diameter. They are stove dried to expel moisture and at the same time the cane acquires a light brown colour. The hollow cane is then split into thin strips, the outsides being smoothed on a belt sander. These are cut to length and tapered, six pieces to each rod, making it hexagonal in cross-section and tapering to a very fine end which has astonishing strength and flexibility.

The six pieces are glued together to form sections about 3ft long, two or sometimes three being joined together to form the rod. The joins may be of brass which slot into one another, or the rod may be taped to hold the sections in position. A cork handle is added and stainless steel fittings are bound on, and the completed rod looks what it is — a work of art.

Farlows of Aberdeen, which bought up the firm of Sharpes some twelve years ago, is probably the biggest concern in Britain making split-cane rods. They turn out about 200 a week — under the trade name of 'Scotties' — exporting about a quarter of these and working overtime to meet a demand which cannot be satisfied.

The only individual making rods single-handed on any significant scale is Rob Wilson, of Brora. He does not have the time to produce very many, unfortunately, but his rods are much sought after by the connoisseur and are valued as collector's pieces.

Megan Boyd, BEM, of Brora, is acknowledged to be the world's best tyer of Salmon fishing flies

Fishing Flies

The Highlands and Islands abound with famous salmon rivers and innumerable lochs where the trout fishing is excellent. The huge demand for fishing flies is hard to meet, though Hong Kong has come to the rescue and is beginning to supply some of the market. A keen fisherman may have about 100 different flies — each one can last for years or it might be lost with the first cast if it catches a snag. There is hardly a business left which makes them in quantity, but a considerable number of individuals supply them to fishing tackle shops. On the other hand many fishermen make their own and get great satisfaction from hooking a fish on a fly they have made. An individual who makes flies for his personal use does so for pleasure rather than economy. A special fly-tying vice is essential, and he must buy

The barrel of a sporting gun is repaired by Douglas Campbell of Aberdeen

hooks and a wide selection of coloured feathers, hair, thread, tinsel and so on.

In the Highlands there is one outstanding maker of salmon flies: Megan Boyd, of Brora in Sutherland, who was awarded the British Empire Medal for fly tying and for teaching the art free of charge to children and the disabled. She makes 100 different flies, her chief reference being Pryce-Tannat's *How to Dress Salmon Flies*, published in 1914. She obtains most of her materials from Veniards of London, who almost monopolise the supplies. Each fly takes up to half an hour to make; one of the more complicated has thirty-four different pieces.

She strives for perfection and her workmanship is superb; she makes flies for royalty and each is a collector's item — yet, curiously, she has never fished herself. She says it takes five years to become any good. The amount of mail she receives asking for flies is an embarrassment and there is a two-year wait for delivery. She was once told, 'Never advertise your work. Let your work advertise you.' By sticking to this principle she has acquired a world-wide reputation; as one American standard work puts it: 'The best flies are made in Scotland and Megan Boyd is acknowledged the best.'

The Gunsmith

Shotguns and rifles are widely used in the Highlands; some of them by the Forestry Commission to shoot deer that manage to penetrate their plantations of young trees, others privately owned for shooting deer, grouse, ptarmigan and blackcock. A pair of top-class guns will cost several thousand pounds; these are superbly made works of art and become valuable family possessions.

Neglect rather than excessive use is the enemy of the gun; if well maintained, it will not often go wrong, while a worn-out barrel can be replaced. Occasionally a gun is damaged or parts wear out — often at an inconvenient moment during a short period of shooting in the Highlands when the owner wants it repaired without delay. Sometimes spare parts are available and are put on a plane from London or Edinburgh, but frequently they have to be hurriedly made by a very skilled craftsman — and it is then that the gun is sent to Anderson and Campbell, of Aberdeen.

Douglas Campbell has a well-fitted workshop stocked with replacement barrels and a heap of spare parts accumulated over the years, and a mass of rifles and shotguns awaiting repairs. There are a number of lathes and drills for making replacement parts on the premises. The only repairers in the north, the firm is inundated with work and has a fine reputation to maintain.

13 Weapons and Instruments

Highland Fighting Equipment

Reproductions of Highland fighting equipment are much in demand for displays, ornamentation and for exhibition in museums. It is of prime importance that the weaponry should be made accurately and in the authentic material; this means

A targe — a tooled leather shield studded with brass — is made by Hugh Ferguson

that the craftsmen who have turned their hands to this task need to be very versatile, working in steel, wood and leather. One such man is Hugh Ferguson of Dornock, a trained silver-smith whose skills cover a wide range.

The most decorative item is the leather targe, a circular wooden shield covered in tooled leather, ornamented with brass studs set in an attractive pattern and a centre boss or spike. Weapons include the claymore, a heavy two-handed sword with a finely tempered blade. This was superseded by the broadsword with a basket hilt; this is made from accurately reproduced master copies cast in several pieces and carefully soldered together — a week's work. Some blades are acid engraved. There are also daggers and dirks with ornamental handles and blades, as well as the *sgain dubh* worn in the stocking of the right leg, which is a general purpose knife rather than a fighting weapon.

These reproduction weapons are sent to Scotsmen all over the world; together with kilts and bagpipes, they serve as treasured mementoes of their homeland.

Bagpipes

One of the most stirring experiences is to listen to the pipers of a Highland regiment in full flow. A solitary piper too can evoke an emotional response in many people. The widespread popularity of the pipes has been typified in recent years by the top-of-the-pops success of 'Amazing Grace'.

The great Highland bagpipe has retained its present form for the last 300 years. A set consists of the bag, covered in tartan; three drones, one bass and two tenor; a chanter, on which the tune is played, and a blowpipe to inflate the bag. The instrument's distinctive feature is the bag itself; this is usually made of sheepskin, with the smooth side innermost, two bags normally being obtained from one sheep. More rarely it is of cowhide. Plastic and rubber have so far proved unsatisfactory for this purpose.

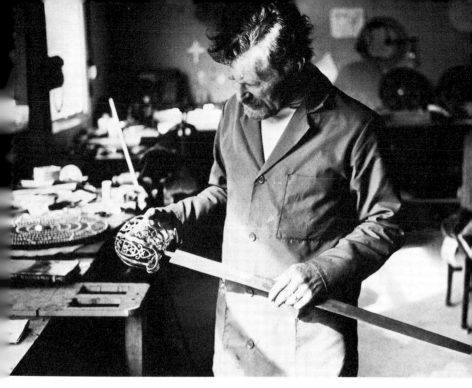

Authentic in every respect, a newly made broadsword

A set of bagpipes is tested; on the right, a drone is adjusted to the
required key

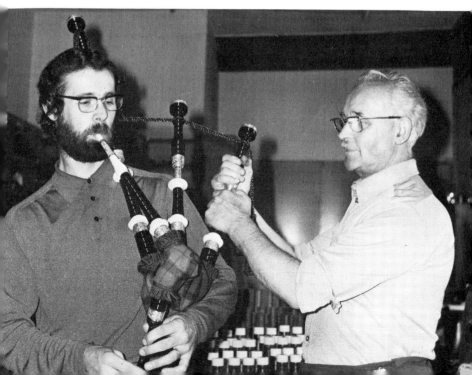

The bag is carefully sewn by hand, using waxed linen thread thicker than the needle, so that the holes are completely filled and the finished bag is airtight, though leather remains slightly porous. The stocks of the drones are fitted by pushing them through from the inside of the bag and binding them securely with waxed thread. The top sections of the drones are later screwed to the stocks. Each drone is fitted with a reed, and the two pieces comprising the drone can be tuned to alter the key when playing.

The chanter has eight holes on which the tune is played with the fingers. Once inflated by means of the blowpipe, the bag is held under the left arm and, to maintain an even note while playing, the action is: blow — squeeze, blow — squeeze.

A set of tassels holds the drones and adds a decorative touch. The fittings are fashioned out of African blackwood, beautifully turned by hand to a very smooth finish and then varnished over. The embellishments, which are purely ornamental and do not affect the playing, are of silver or ivory. In earlier times laburnum wood and staghorn were used. The fittings last indefinitely and are often handed down from father to son. Depending on how much they are used and the care taken to look after them, the bags themselves may remain serviceable for many years; a special seasoning preparation has to be poured inside to help preserve them.

Although the bagpipes are a Highland instrument, there are none being made in the area, the principal makers being in Glasgow, Edinburgh and Forfar. It is the ambition of all serious pipers to own a set with hand-chased silver fittings, which can cost around £500. The pipes look particularly attractive when ivory is used to highlight the silver. Sets made of imitation ivory are perfectly adequate, however, and much less expensive at about £100. But, with rising costs of materials and labour, these prices are bound to increase.

Many sets are exported, principally to Scotsmen living abroad, though they are also, rather surprisingly, popular in Denmark. One firm sends about a hundred a year to Brittany where they are played in conjunction with a local instrument, a kind of clarinet, called a 'bombard'.

The pipes, which are of ancient origin, are still played in parts of the Mediterranean, and emigrating Scotsmen have taken their traditional bagpipes to every corner of the world, many countries having their pipe bands. But nowhere does the playing of them equal the skill and fervour of the Scottish piper.

The serious player has to practise every day. There are some professional pipers, who may be teachers or competitors at the Highland gatherings. These are sometimes sponsored by firms and prize money is being stepped up. Beginners can use a practice chanter, which is easy to blow, and then graduate to a proper set in a few months. The playing of pipes is now an 'O' level subject in Scottish schools, which will give an impetus to the craft of making them.

Fiddles

The fiddle is another important musical instrument in these regions. Most crofts possessed one, which was handed down as an heirloom. It was probably of foreign make and brought home by returning fishermen. The fiddle was produced on all festive occasions, such as weddings and family celebrations, and a special type of folk music was played.

In the Shetlands the fiddle takes precedence over the bagpipes and children are learning to play it at school. Aly Bain of Lerwick plays the fiddle all over the world and makes recordings.

There is a general shortage of instruments, partly due to the expense of a good one, and there are very few craftsmen to make them. In Lerwick, Alec Leask does not produce many new instruments but his workmanship is superb. He has retired and fiddle making is his hobby, though in fact he mostly does repairs for people when they resurrect an old instrument and want to play it. There has been an enormous renewal of interest in the fiddle and it is being played by many more people.

A fiddle is made with a pine front and maple back, the material being obtained from firms specialising in wood for musical instruments. The curved front and back are each fashioned from a single piece of wood, which is not bent but carved to shape with chisel and gouge until it is about ⅛in thick. This requires great concentration and frequent use of callipers — one slip could ruin the whole operation. Inside the instrument is a sound bar — left when the wood is whittled away — and a vertical sound post is fitted later. The maker always signs and dates the fiddle on the inside. It is stuck together with animal glue, so that it can be taken apart for repair at any time. About a dozen coats of varnish are applied to give a perfect finish. The bridge, chin rest and strings are bought as required. A new instrument takes time to settle and mature, and improves with playing.

A fiddle — traditionally there was one in every croft — being made by Alec Leask

14 Artist Crafts

Glassblowing

Some of the most important producers of quality glassware anywhere in Britain are located in the Highlands, where young and enthusiastic local inhabitants have become skilled in the art of glassblowing. One company specialising in individually created pieces, notably paperweights of original design, is Caithness Glass Ltd, of Wick. Its success has been meteoric and it continues to expand. It was started in 1960 to create employment, and glassblowers from abroad were brought in to give instruction. Only one of them remains; the rest of the work is done by local men who have attained a high degree of proficiency. It takes about four years to become a good glassblower and the skill improves with experience.

The main ingredient of glass is silica which is obtained from sand. Lochaline in Argyll, opposite the island of Mull, has just the right sand for glassmaking. The silica is melted and other ingredients — soda, potash and lead in the form of lead oxide — are added. This makes a heavy, brilliant and comparatively soft glass that is ideal for blowing. The glass is heated to a high temperature in a crucible inside a furnace. An assistant dips a hollow blowing iron, some 5ft long, into the molten glass and withdraws it with a bobble of glass on the end, keeping the rod turning so that it is evenly distributed.

The iron is handed to the glassblower who sits in his chair and shapes the glass, using a mould in the shape of a half circle. He then stands up and commences to blow; the glass expands

like a balloon and, during the later stages, it is blown into a mould to give the right shape. From time to time his creation is put in a special furnace to heat but not melt it, and it can be dipped into another crucible containing glass of a different colour. When a handle is needed, a piece of glass is quickly and skilfully attached and shaped. At each stage the working temperature is important, particularly at the moment when the rod is tapped to detach the completed article. It is then cooled over a period of about eight hours to avoid stresses, after which it is inspected and finished by grinding smooth any sharp edges.

Caithness Glass is particularly well known for its paperweights which are also made at the firm's works in Oban where these are the sole product. The Caithness designs are original, colourful, abstract and futuristic. The company's success lies in being able to produce these bizarre effects in quantity while each individual item is slightly different. Most of the finer points of these processes are a closely guarded secret.

Starting with a piece of molten glass on a rod, coloured flowers or other motifs are attached to a glass ball which is then dipped into molten liquid glass so that the ball with its attachments are encased in an outer coating of glass. This is left to cool for a day, then carefully inspected and the base is ground flat.

One man can turn out thirty of the simpler kind in a day — there is also a woman who makes paperweights; but only one or two of the more complicated designs can be made in the same working time, on top of which there is significant wastage, though this is not necessarily the fault of the craftsman.

The Caithness paperweights of special design are changing hands at greatly increased prices as they are much in demand by collectors and will doubtless become the valuable antiques of tomorrow, especially when designed by Colin Terris.

Glassblowing at the Caithness works

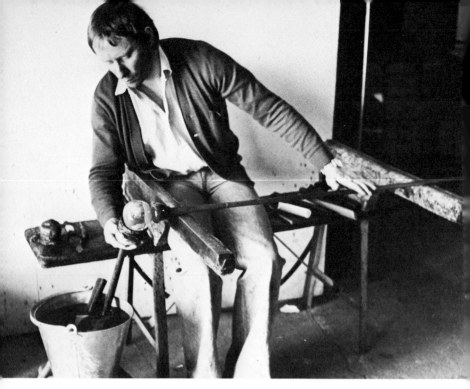

Peter Holmes making a paperweight, a speciality of Caithness Glass

Engraving glass by means of a copper wheel at Caithness

Another important concern is Perthshire Paperweights Ltd, of Crieff, which borders on the old line of the Highlands. Their craftsmen are specialists in the traditional millefiori type of paperweight (in which coloured rods are fused together to produce an attractive pattern) and steadily gaining an international reputation, notably in the United States. Also in Crieff is the well-known Strathearn Glass Company which makes paperweights and a wide variety of blown glassware.

Glass Engraving

This takes two forms — copperwheel engraving and sand-blasting. The first process involves holding the piece of glass against a copperwheel rotating at high speed. The wheel varies in diameter from around 2in to a mere pinhead size. Normally the design is drawn on the glass with a felt-tipped pen in order to get the spacing right and allow for the curvature of the glass as well as the fact that the sides are rarely parallel. The wheel is charged with abrasive, the craftsman puts on his protective goggles and engraving commences.

The work is tiring and difficult, for the engraving is often most detailed and exact, and the article may be an awkward shape to work on. It has to be held to the wheel and moved around to cut the pattern; by cutting deeper a three-dimensional effect is achieved. The engraver's concentration cannot be relaxed at any stage.

The demand for high-class work is huge, with many individual orders for presentation purposes and gifts, and the talented team of artists who do glass engraving at Caithness are kept fully occupied.

The most famous glass engraver in the Highlands is doubtless Harold Gordon, of Forres. When he set up business on his own in 1948 he was the only full-time copperwheel glass engraver in Britain and his reputation has grown steadily. His skill at his craft combined with his drawing ability and good taste have ensured a demand for his pieces. Using a diamond pointed pen

he meticulously engraves his signature on the base of each individual piece.

Sand blasting is a quicker process. The pattern to be engraved is cut out of a piece of adhesive material and stuck on the glass. A jet of sand is directed on to it, care being taken not to overdo it as a hole can be bored in the glass in a very short time. By this means the pattern is engraved on the glass.

Pottery

Artist potters, a large percentage of them from England, have in recent years been encouraged by grants and loans to set up business in the Highlands. Their hand-thrown products, thanks to good workmanship, tasteful design and attractive finish, have found favour with the public and are selling profitably.

There are also larger concerns, such as Castlewynd Studios at Kingussie, formerly at Aviemore, and the Highland Pottery at Lochinver, which is bursting at the seams and on the move to Ullapool, as well as a smaller one at Lybster. These employ local labour and use volume methods of producing pottery — pressing out such items as plates and making use of moulds. In moulding, a solution of clay and water — or slip — is poured into plaster-of-Paris moulds and when, after a certain time, the slip is poured out again a $\frac{1}{4}$in-thick impression remains inside. As this dries, it shrinks and can be removed quite easily, the mould usually being in two halves.

The articles made by this method are finished by craftsmen who add handles, and so on, before they are fired in the kiln. After the first firing, the artists get to work on the glazing and decoration, the colour and design playing an important part in attracting the eye of the buyer.

The craftsman potter works differently, each item being 'thrown' on the wheel and individually raised by hand. The clay is first prepared by pugging and wedging to get it into the right condition, by mixing it up, dispersing any lumps and

Harold Gordon engraving glass at Forres

adding water to obtain an even consistency. Supplies of suitable clay come from England, in most cases from Stoke on Trent.

Then a piece is cut off and weighed; this the potter throws on his revolving wheel — usually electrically driven — and skilfully shapes with his hands. When making a range or set of similar pots, bowls, cups or other items, he has to take care to achieve the same height, curve and thickness. Each article is fired twice: the first time to the 'biscuit' state; then, after being dipped in glaze and decorated, it is put in the kiln for a second firing. With fuel costs so high, the kiln is packed with as many items as possible, the duration and temperature of the firing being an important part of the operation.

The amount of time the potter spends at his wheel is very small compared with the hours taken up with preparation and finishing. But many are reluctant to employ an assistant who, as soon as he has become proficient, tends to move on and set up on his own. The potter builds his reputation over a period of years, striving to perfect his individual style of design and colouring. Most potters have their own shops; others sell to wholesalers whence their products find their way to the craft shops. The successful craftsman potter needs to combine his artistic skills with a practical turn of mind that will enable him to be an efficient businessman and packer of his finished work.

Silverwork

In the past decade silversmithing has increased in importance, particularly in the Islands. There is a large output of reasonably priced and attractively designed articles to be seen in all the craft shops and a good percentage goes for export. Items of Celtic and Norse design are popular, and so are pieces with a Scottish association, such as thistles, birds and animals.

To make a single item of jewellery, like a brooch, works out very expensive owing to the time involved in cutting it from a

Decorating pottery at Lochinver

sheet of silver. So a master is made of a particular design and this is cast by the 'lost wax' method. This enables an individual piece to be produced in quantity and so keeps the price to a reasonable level.

The first step in casting is to make a mould; this is done by putting the master pattern between sheets of rubber which are vulcanised by heat and pressure. The mould is carefully cut open, the master removed and a channel cut to allow the wax to be poured in. This is done by machine with the mould closed up. The wax impression is then removed from the mould and attached to a tree — this can take about a hundred small-item impressions. A cylinder, called a 'flask', is placed over the tree and filled with plaster of Paris which is allowed to harden. The flask is heated, and the wax melts and flows out. The flask is then placed in a centrifuge with a crucible of molten silver in the centre; as the flask is revolved at speed, the silver is forced into all parts of the mould. The plaster of Paris is then removed, leaving the silver patterns attached to the tree. These are detached and inspected for flaws, then smoothed off and polished.

As they are of silver, they have to be hallmarked and are sent to Edinburgh for this to be done. On return, the finishing touches and polishing are carried out to complete the work. By using this method, a quantity of identical articles are produced, which is essential when selling wholesale.

Many of the designers who have become interested in silver-work began by doing it part time as a money-making hobby, but their natural skill coupled with the demand for their work turned an individually practised craft into a thriving small industry. In the Orkneys, Ola Gorie in Kirkwall, and 'Ortak', just outside the town, are two firms which have prospered. 'Ortak' and, in the Shetlands, Shetland Silverware have built larger workshops and employ girl assistants. On the mainland, at Inverness, John Frazer, who has probably been established the longest, has acquired a reputation for the excellence of his work; while farther south, at Fort William, 'Magnus Maximus' is also successful. All of them can work in gold as well, though there is not much demand for such products.

One outstanding silversmith, who works on individual pieces of the highest quality, is Malcolm Appleby. He started as a gun engraver and set up his business at Crathes Station working in silver and gold which he engraves superbly. Such is his fame that he is inundated with orders and can choose which he will undertake. He recently made a chess set for a London firm, the pieces carved from whales' teeth and set in gold and silver. His talent and versatility have made him one of the foremost craftsmen in Britain.

One of Britain's foremost craftsmen, Malcolm Appleby, works in silver and gold at his Crathes Station workshop

Pewterware

Pewter — a metal composed of tin, lead and copper — was much used in earlier times to make household articles like tankards and dishes. Today it lends itself well to the production of bracelets, brooches, pendants and other ornamental items on sale in many craft shops. As pewter is a good deal less expensive than silver, these can be bought at a comparatively reasonable price.

Foremost in the field is Fountain of Dornoch, which has acquired a reputation for good workmanship and design. With half a dozen workers, output is quite large but not enough to satisfy demand.

Patterns of the particular article are cut from a sheet of pewter, and the decorating is done with a hammer and die — a method called 'striking and stamping'. They are finished by filing and polishing on a wheel, and are ultrasonically cleaned and polished in a chemical solution. From this treatment they emerge bright and shining. Holes or fittings are then made, ready to take brooch pins or chains, which are bought in from suppliers. Finally the articles are lacquered and fired to preserve the shine and prevent tarnishing.

Some items are individually made, but because of the work involved and the original design these carry a higher price. This is acceptable for presentation pieces but not for the whole-sale market which is the bread and butter of the business. All artist craftsmen are faced with this state of affairs — having to produce what the public wants and not what they would like to create.

The method of 'striking and stamping' pewter with a hammer and die is demonstrated by Charles Fountain, of Dornoch

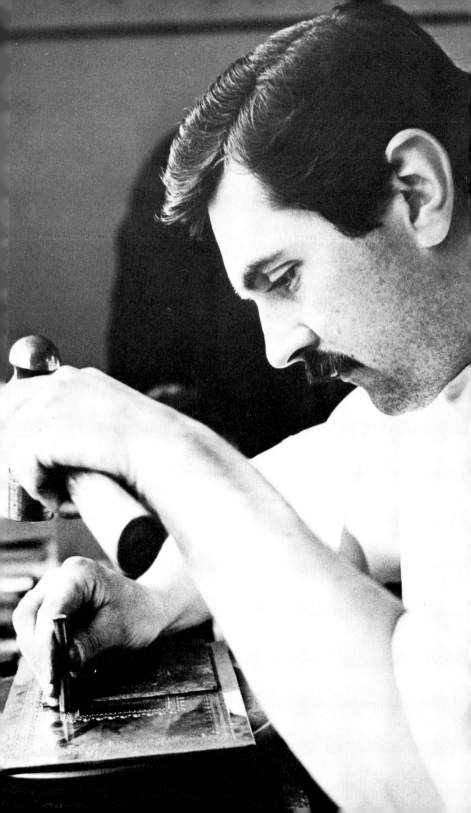

Bookbinding

Fine workmanship is required for high-class bookbinding in all its aspects. This entails such skilled operations as stitching, backing and rounding, the marbling or gilding of page edges, binding in best Morocco leather and lettering in gold leaf. One firm in the north of Scotland whose craftsmen carry out this varied work is George Jolly, of Aberdeen. This 100-year-old establishment is kept busy meeting the demand not only for binding new books but for renovating and re-covering cherished volumes in libraries or private collections. Books may be attacked by woodworm or damaged by damp; even in well-ventilated rooms leather bindings can deteriorate or become dried up and need reviving. Family correspondence or records of historical interest may turn up in an attic and be collected into specially bound volumes. One particular line is a range of prestige ledgers and account books which are produced most elegantly for an old-established firm of accountants and some of the new oil companies. Thanks to its excellent reputation in bringing the craft of bookbinding to a fine art, this Aberdeen firm has plenty of top quality work on its hands.

Enamelling

Enamelling work on copper, silver and gold is done by a few artist craftsmen, whose output is much in demand.

Their equipment includes a small oven with an accurate temperature control, as the degree of heat is most critical in the firing process. Also needed is the special enamelling paint in a range of colours; this is ground into powder form and some enamellers do this themselves.

To make a copper ash tray, for example, the metal is bought already saucer-shaped. This is heated in the furnace and then pickled in acid to clean it up. When cool, the inside is coated

Marbling the page-ends of a book, one aspect of the fine art of bookbinding

with gum arabic; a colour base in powder form is dusted over this and adheres to the gum. During firing, the powder melts and colours the article. It is cooled and then hardens.

If any additional decoration is required, gum arabic is painted on in the chosen design and variegated coloured crystals, in the form of 'hundreds and thousands', are sprinkled on. These adhere to the gum and, by means of a pointed tool like a pencil, are quickly spaced out. The ash tray is fired again for a few minutes and, when just right, the colours melt. These can then, if desired, be stirred with a metal tool into a twirling pattern similar to that of marbling paper.

When removed from the oven, the ash tray is left to harden once more and then finally finished. Small items like bangles and rings can also be decorated in this way.

The final products are most attractive, the patterns and colours varying from purely decorative to miniature pictures, according to the individual artist's design.

Commander Norman, model maker of Strathpeffer, at work reparing an antique pair of bellows

Model Making

A model maker's skill lies in his ability to work to scale, often in microscopic dimensions, in producing accurate miniatures of a wide variety of objects. One of Britain's foremost exponents is Commander Norman, of Strathpeffer, who was employed by the Admiralty as a model maker after retiring from the Royal Navy. Mostly pieces for museums or exhibitions, his model ships are built with meticulous care and precision from detailed plans, and measure anything from a few inches to 2-3ft long.

The work is done in wood and metal, using a battery of tools and a lathe that can cope with the construction of miniature items in smallest detail. He also does carving and inlay work, makes *sgain dubhs* — knives used by Highlanders — and restores articles that have been given up as beyond repair, such as the bellows shown in the photograph.

Ships in Bottles

The sight of a model ship inside a bottle has been a source of fascination to children ever since the art was first practised many years ago. Adults, too, may well wonder how ships get into bottles. It is a time-consuming task and few of these handicrafts reach the shops. They are mostly made by retired seamen as a money-making sideline and are much in demand. Donald Mackintosh, of Peterhead, turns out about four a week, each taking up to twenty hours. His wife's delicate touch is helpful with the finer pieces.

The bottles are fairly easy to obtain, dimpled ones being preferred as these do not roll about. The model may be of a sailing ship or fishing boat; occasionally someone will ask for a reproduction in miniature of his own yacht. The hull is carved out of pine; the sails are made of nylon cloth, the spars of broom bristles, and the rigging of fine cotton thread. The masts are fashioned so that they pivot and lie flat, to enable the model to be passed through the neck of the bottle.

With the bottle lying on its side, coloured plasticine — representing the sea — is pressed along the base, using surgeon's pincers. The model is carefully manoeuvred inside and set firmly on the plasticine so that it is held securely. The masts and sails are then pulled upright by using the pincers and pulling on the lengths of cotton that form the rigging. When all is shipshape, a drop of glue secures the cotton thread to the bows; after this has dried, the surplus threads are cut, the bottle sealed and the work of art is complete.

Craftsmen at Work

A considerable number of artist craftsmen welcome visitors to their workshops. In some of the larger establishments, special arrangements are made, facilities being particularly good at the Caithness and Oban glassworks, where glassblowers can be seen at work; at some weaving concerns, such as Loch Carron Weavers; and a few silversmiths and potters, as well as the Balnakiel Crafts Centre, near Durness in Sutherland.

Blacksmiths, though few and far between, may be seen working in their smithies, and boatbuilders at yards around the coast. Coopers and saddlers it is advisable to visit by appointment. Farriers, thatchers and dry stone wallers are fairly mobile and may be seen in action only by chance. In some instances, where rural craftsmen work anonymously and are remotely situated, visitors — particularly if they arrive in force — may not be entirely welcome.

Some whisky distilleries invite visitors to look round. In the Spey Valley area, the AA have signposted the 'Whisky Trail'. Glenfarclas-Glenlivet, near Ballindalloch, in Banffshire, have a small museum and provide a guided tour of the premises — with a 'wee dram' at the end of it.

Watermills which may be viewed include the click mill at Dounby, in the Orkneys; rather remotely situated, it has been restored and has a horizontal wheel. There is a mill at Shawbost, on the Isle of Lewis in the Outer Hebrides, and another near Colbost on Skye.

A Visitor's Guide to Scottish Craft Workshops is an invaluable small booklet giving an up-to-date list of all workshops which can be visited and their hours of opening. It can be obtained from the Scottish Development Agency, 102 Telford Road, Edinburgh EH4 2NP.

Appendix 2
Crafts on Display

Scottish craftsmen display their products at two important events held every autumn: the Highland Trade Fair, at Aviemore, organised by the Highlands and Islands Development Board; and the Scottish Crafts Trade Fair, at Ingliston on the outskirts of Edinburgh, organised by the Scottish Development Agency.

Traditional crafts are exhibited in many of the local museums:

Town Museums

Aberdeen:	Provost Skenes House — local history and period furniture
Fort William:	The West Highland Museum — excellent and comprehensive
Inverness:	History museum with some local crafts; Kilt making and museum at 'Kiltmakers', 4-9 Huntly Street
Oban:	A small collection of local interest
Orkneys:	The Tankerness House Museum, Kirkwall, shows crofts and local crafts A small maritime museum at Stromness
Peterhead:	The Arbuthnot Museum — shipping and local crafts
Shetlands:	Shetland County Museum, Lerwick — excellent display of crafts and Shetland way of life

Thurso:	Good coverage of the port of Thurso and Caithness stone
Ullapool:	General interest
Wick:	The Wick Society Museum — coopering display and herring fishing

Croft Museums

Some of the old, restored crofts are rather far afield but well worth a visit. Traditional farm tools, household utensils and furnishings are arranged as they would have been when the croft was originally occupied. The roof construction and method of thatching can also be seen.

Auchindrain, Argyll:	Museum of farm life recently formed from a multiple tenancy farm; a complex of crofts, farm buildings and equipment
Culloden, Inverness-shire:	Furnished croft
Glencoe:	Small museum packed with interest, excellent for the Ballachulish slate industry
Kingussie, Inverness-shire:	The Highland Folk Museum — extensive, with a black house and click mill from Lewis
Latheron, Caithness:	Laidhay Preservation Trust
Dervaig, Mull:	Small private museum of folk life and farm tools
Outer Hebrides:	The Black House, Arnol, Barvas, Isles of Lewis North Uist South Uist, at Eachar
Shetlands:	Boddam, Dunrossness

Skye: Kilmuir Croft Museum
Three Chimneys Museum, Colbost — with
an illicit whisky still

The Landmark visitors' centre at Carrbridge is of general
interest, with its theatre and nature trail; the emphasis is more
on natural history than crafts.

Addresses of Organisations

Scottish Development Agency — Small Business Division (formerly Small Industries Council for Rural Areas of Scotland), 102 Telford Road, Edinburgh EH4 2NP.
This organisation publishes the booklet *A Visitor's Guide to Scottish Craft Workshops*.

The Highlands and Islands Development Board
Bridge House, 27 Bank Street, Inverness.

Scottish Crafts Centre
Acheson House, 140 Canongate, Edinburgh.
A display of craftsmen's high-quality work can always be seen here.

Highland Home Industries
94 George Street, Edinburgh.
This is the headquarters; it has shops in several towns.

Dry Stone Walling Association
Gatehouse of Fleet, Kirkcudbright.

The Harris Tweed Association
6 Garden Road, Stornoway, Isle of Lewis; and Station Square, Inverness.

The Scottish Tourist Board
2 Rutland Place, Edinburgh.

Tourist Information Offices, strategically placed throughout Scotland, are open in the summer months. They give helpful advice and usually advertise local crafts and where craftsmen can be seen at work.

Bibliography

Highland Folk Ways by I. F. Grant (1975)

Rural Crafts in Scotland by James A. Mackay (1976)

Scottish Crafts and Craftsmen by Michael Brander (Edinburgh, 1974)

A Guide to Scottish Whisky by Michael Brander (Edinburgh, 1975)

Explore the Highlands and Islands, a Highlands and Islands Development Board pamphlet

Highland Information Series, a series of pamphlets on all aspects of life in the Highlands, published by An Comunn Gaidhealach, Abertarff House, Inverness

Index

Page numbers in italic type refer to illustrations.

antlers, 44

bagpipes, 12, 96-9, *97*
Ballachulish slates, 27-8, 36
baskets, 33-5, *34*
blacksmith, 23-5, *25*, 119
boatbuilding, 8, 14-17, *15*
bookbinding, 8, *114*, 115
bottles, ships in, 117, 118
buttons, horn, 44

Caithness slabs, 28-9, *28*
carding, 48, 51, 60
chairs, Orkney, 19-22, *21*
cheese, 87-9, *88*
Clearances, 7
coopering, 8, 9, 65-70, *66, 68*, 119
coppersmith, 26
creels, lobsters, 14, 78, *77*
croft museums, 122-3
crofters, 7, 11
crooks, shepherds, 44-5

deerskin, 42
dry stone walls, 12, 30-1, *31, 32*
dykes, dry stone, 30
dyeing, wool, 51

enamelling, 115

farrier, 24-5, *25*, 119
fiddle, 12, 99, 100, *100*
finnan haddock, 76

fish, barrels, 68-70, *69*
    drying, 11, 71, *72*
    finnan haddock, 76
    kippers, 73-5, *75*
    lobsters, 77
    salted herrings, 71-3, *72*
    salmon, 76-7
    smokies, 76
fishing, flies, 91-3, *91*
    rods, 90-1

glass, blowing, 101-3, *102*, 119
    engraving, 104-7, *104, 106*
    paperweights, 103-5, *104*
gunsmith, 92-4, *92*

harness, 39-41, *41*
Harris tweed, 46, 49-54
Hattersley looms, 49, *51*, 52-4
heather thatch, 36
herrings, 8
    salted, 71-3, *72*
hide, 39-42
Highland line, 7
horn, 42, 44-5

kilts, 62-4, *63*
kippers, 73-5, *75*
knitting, 48, 54-61, *55, 57, 59, 61*

lobster creels, 77-8, *77*
looms, 49, *51*-2

malt whisky, 26, *85*
malting barley, 82-5
milling wool, 48
   corn, 81-4, *84*
modelmaking, 116-17, *116*
museums, 121-3

oil, 8
Orkney chairs, 19-22, *21*
   baskets, 33-5, *34*

peat, 12, 80-3, *81, 82, 83*
pewter, 112-13, *113*
Portsoy marble, 30
pottery, 107-9, *109*, 119

quern, 12

rooing, 58
rope, 35-6

saddlery, 9, 39-41, *40, 41*, 119
seaweed, 46, 78-9
sgain dubh, 96, 117
shawls, Shetland, 58-61, *59, 61*
sheep, 46, 58
sheepskins, 41-3, *43*

ships in bottles, 117-18
silverwork, 108, 110-11, *111*, 119
smokies, 76
spinning, 8, 11, *47*, 56, 60
spinning wheels, 12, *47*, 49-51, 60
sport, fishing flies, 91-3, *91*
   fishing rods, 90-1
   gunsmith, 92-4, *92*
stone, 12, 27-32, *28, 31*, 38
stone walls, 11-12, 30-2, *31, 32*,
   119
straw work, 20-2, *34*

tartan, 62
template, 30
thatching, 8, 11, 36-8, *37, 38*, 119
turning wood, 18

walls, stone, 11-12, 29, 30-2, *31,*
   32, 119
watermill, 119
weapons, 95-7, *95, 97*
weaving, 8, 11, 48-54, *49*, 119
whisky, 9, 26, 84-7, *85*, 119
whisky barrels, 65-8, *66*
woodworkers, 18-22, *19, 20, 21*
wool, 46-61, *46*